To Dennis,

Keep Riding and

Go Argyle!

ARGYLE ARMADA

ARGYLE ARMADA

BEHIND THE SCENES OF THE PRO CYCLING LIFE

ARMADA

MARK JOHNSON

BOULDER, COLORADO

3002 Sterling Circle, Suite 100
Boulder, Colorado 80301-2338 USA
(303) 440-0601 · Fax (303) 444-6788 · E-mail velopress@competitorgroup.com

Distributed in the United States and Canada by Ingram Publisher Services

A Cataloging-in-Publication record for this book is available from the Library of Congress.
ISBN 978-1-934030-81-3

For information on purchasing VeloPress books,
please call (800) 811-4210 ext. 2138 or visit www.velopress.com.

Cover and interior design by Erin Johnson
Composition by Erin Johnson and Vicki Hopewell
Cover and interior photographs by Mark Johnson, except pages
41, 88, 95 (bottom), 97 (bottom), 140 (top), and 147 by Cor Vos

Text set in Warnock Pro Light

12 13 14 / 10 9 8 7 6 5 4 3 2 1

CONTENTS

FOREWORD

It was the best of times, it was the worst of times.
—*Charles Dickens,* A Tale of Two Cities

"Hey, wow . . . ummm . . . hey, are you Jonathan Vaughters?" was the first thing I heard as I thumped into my seat for the long flight back to Denver from Paris this past July. At first I thought I had sat in the wrong seat or left my passport somewhere (again), but my not-so-silent admirer quickly told me all about how big a fan of the team he was, and how great 2011 had been, and how cool argyle was, and how awesome . . .

I was flattered, but this was the first of many circumstances that made me realize how the outside world viewed Garmin-Cervélo's 2011 season. It created a much bigger stir than I would ever have ventured to guess.

I say "outside world" because when you are directing a race like the Tour, you are submersed in a microsociety that lacks big-picture perspective on the outside world. In my little world, 2011 had been a constant and nasty battle, a tightrope act with no net and no forgiveness. Of course, I had celebrated and appreciated the victories, but I was always all too aware that professional cycling is a game of "What have you done for me lately?" It took this overly enthusiastic fellow passenger to make me realize that most people had looked at our 2011 as a dream season.

The dissonance between my 2011 and that of the broader world was tied up in the knowledge of how many difficult decisions had to be made through the year. And how each and every one of those decisions also carried the possibility of throwing the entire 2011 season into the bin if they were interpreted the wrong way or didn't have the intended outcome. We had a unique team in 2011, one with many top-tier riders but without any definitive super talent like an Alberto Contador or a Philippe Gilbert. Our strength was always in our numbers and in our ability to play a calculated and cold game, one that flew in the face of cycling traditions. And, as is often the case, our strength was almost our undoing. While playing a tight, numerical game may be highly effective, it does not lend itself to satisfying individual objectives and personal goals. No one individual gets his way, which inevitably leads to tension. That tension was the reality of 2011.

Of course, tension is the common currency for all cycling teams and seasons. A cycling team is always an odd compromise among many parties. Riders have their individual ambitions, sponsors have their ideals and goals, the rules of the game and tradition have their pull on the agenda, the press has its loud opinion, and somewhere caught in the middle of all this rests the team. And specifically, the team manager. Not to diminish the role of the team, but the final decision as to how to execute the great compromise that makes up every choice in cycling rests with that individual.

Decision-making ability is what I've heard people refer to as power. Yet power was not what I felt in so many situations over the year. Instead of power, I felt the immense weight of responsibility before every decision I made. In each case, someone would be upset. Maybe a rider, maybe the press, maybe the fans, maybe a sponsor. Accepting and

dealing with their upset is part of the responsibility of power, I suppose. Furthermore, what many don't realize is that after I made a hard decision, I felt totally powerless as I watched the inevitable consequences unfold. Even when you win, the consequences of these decisions roll on, in the media and in the minds of fans. The consequences are yours for life, and once you've made your final choice, you are powerless to change the consequences.

So, for me, instead of a glory-filled romp, 2011 was a series of lonely and difficult decisions followed by anxiety as I awaited the results. From folding the former Cervélo TestTeam and its riders into our squad to allowing Johan Vansummeren to go ahead in Roubaix to leaving him and Dan Martin at home for the Tour de France. From the misconstrued "don't chase" order in Flanders to infamously leaving Thor Hushovd off the Vuelta squad. Each and every choice balanced the interests of the riders, the sponsors, the UCI, fans, media, and investors. That's what I remember about 2011.

While this may seem a melancholy assessment for such a brilliant year, making tough choices is where I find my pride. Each and every time, in retrospect and maturity, the hard and often unpopular decisions proved to be the decisions that were best for the team as a whole. There is a certain satisfaction in taking harsh criticism in the moment, swallowing hard and accepting the blows, and then being proven correct with the passage of time.

As I sit here in December and look back at 2011, I realize how many impossibly difficult and unpredictable decisions we had to make and how most of them turned out exactly as we hoped. And right there is why I feel a true sense of success. It's not the performances or the wins unto themselves that make me know 2011 was our best season; it's the process that went into creating those wins—the decisions that went into them. Above all, it's knowing that the process that led to wins is on solid ground for the future. That brings sound sleep, in a way that lucky wins never do.

When you're in the middle of so much movement, it's difficult to reflect properly and understand each event and each accomplishment. I remember riding with the guys down the Champs-Élysées on our victory lap; was I thinking about what an incredible Tour we'd just had? Sadly, no. Instead, I was daydreaming about what we needed to do to make it better in 2012. It's the nature of cycling: Never look back. That said, I hope this book and these memories will allow me a bit of storytelling peace someday. Cycling is such a magnificently gorgeous sport that to not stand back and look at it, for all of what it is and what it represents, would be tragic. While I've got next year to deal with now, I'm sure you'll enjoy this trip through Slipstream's finest year so far.

—*Jonathan Vaughters*

In 2007, someone from Slipstream Sports, the holding company that owns Team Garmin-Cervélo, e-mailed me to license some bike racing photographs. Matt Johnson, the team's recently hired president, was putting together proposals for potential sponsors. Some of my photos, as well as some wordsmithing, went into a pitch that ended up on the desk of Jon Cassat, Garmin's vice president of communications. A few months later, the Kansas City–based company hitched its name to Jonathan Vaughters's young bike team.

Three years later, net revenue from Garmin's fitness division had grown to eclipse that of its mammoth automotive GPS division. Although it's difficult to draw a conclusive correlation between any marketing investment and an increase in sales, it's no stretch to say that from the day Garmin's pro cycling team hit the headlines at the 2008 Tour de France (where Christian Vande Velde placed fourth overall), the company's GPS devices were suddenly on the radar of cyclists, triathletes, runners, and active people around the planet.

Neither Slipstream nor Garmin commissioned this book, but it is nevertheless an outgrowth of my long relationship with the team as a freelance writer and photographer. As I wrote and took pictures throughout the 2011 season, I tried to let the constellation of voices surrounding the Garmin-Cervélo team, along with the riders' actions, tell the story of the scenes behind the pro cycling life.

By collecting opinions, observations, and moments in the lives of the team riders, race organizers, Slipstream staff and executives, UCI officials, and many more, my intent was to disappear behind the scenery and let the story take form through the shaping forces of a collection of pro cycling characters. Along the way, the business of cycling emerged as a recurring topic, and you'll find it a steady motif throughout this book. This is a fascinating reality of the nature of Jonathan Vaughters's project. Vaughters, the team's founder and CEO, feels that professional cycling's social and financial fragility is perplexingly incongruous with the sport's bedrock-deep public popularity and stability. That opinion shapes his perceptive view of the sport's history and long-term potential.

In the United States alone, you would need to combine all the country's snow skiers, tennis players, and golfers to match the nation's burgeoning population of regular cyclists. And in Europe, where social rides draw huge crowds (for example, the Tour of Flanders sportif sees more than 20,000 cyclists show up at dawn to ride the cobbled lanes of Belgium), the sport is becoming even more deeply woven into the fabric of daily life. As one crusty old Belgian gent grunted from astride his steel-tubed racing bike while watching the Garmin-Cervélo riders pick their way through crowds to the start of a Wednesday race called Brabantse Pijl, "Ooof. It didn't used to be this way—it's getting too popular."

It is that growing popularity that makes the current era so critical for the future of bicycle racing, and in this book I've attempted to show how the riders' on-the-road racing dramas intersect with the organizational challenges Vaughters faces as he tries to reform pro cycling. Vaughters is an entrepreneur, a person who dedicates himself to an audacious project with singular, life-consuming focus. He sincerely wants to make racing better. But in a sport where tradition often trumps both common sense and the restlessly inventive, often mercantile values Vaughters was born into in the United States, his little band of racing cyclists is representative of both pro cycling's tomorrows and the traumas of today—turmoil that shakes the sport as it evolves from its cloistered European roots and becomes a truly international sporting spectacle.

The process of writing and shooting a book like this in the midst of a pro bike team for a year is a bit like being a jellyfish: You hang around waiting for bits and pieces to float into your tentacles. As Tom Danielson exclaimed upon seeing me in Colorado Springs not long after the team's Tour de France celebration on the Champs-Élysées, "You are everywhere!" I tried to be, although I admit that, for the team, having a jellyfish around wasn't always comfortable. As such, my most profound thanks to the Garmin-Cervélo riders and staff for graciously opening the doors of the team's buses, hotels, and cars for the entire season. The same goes for Jonathan Vaughters, team president Matt Johnson, and team owner Doug Ellis, all of whom patiently fielded my inquiries throughout the year and granted me an astonishing degree of trust. Without the team's patience and good humor, this book would not exist.

A photographer can't be everywhere at once. So thank you also to legendary Dutch photographer Cor Vos for the use of his images of Dan Martin winning stage 9 of the Vuelta, Sep Vanmarcke climbing out of a ravine at the same race, Johan Vansummeren on the Roubaix cobbles, and one of the Tour of California podium shots. Thanks also to ThinkTank for supplying me with camera bags. My ThinkTank gear took an astounding amount of travel abuse while shooting this book, and the thoughtful design and stout build of ThinkTank products never ceased to amaze me.

Most of all, thanks to my wife, Melinda, and sons, Sammy and Nico. They saw too little of me during my year creating this book, and I dedicate it to them.

—Mark Johnson

CAST OF CHARACTERS

Principal Team Garmin-Cervélo members mentioned in this text:

MEN'S TEAM

Jack Bobridge
Tom Danielson
Julian Dean
Thomas Dekker
Tyler Farrar
Murilo Fischer
Roger Hammond
Heinrich Haussler
Ryder Hesjedal
Thor Hushovd
Andreas Klier
Michel Kreder
Brett Lancaster
Christophe Le Mével
Daniel Lloyd
Martijn Maaskant
Dan Martin
Cam Meyer
Travis Meyer
David Millar
Ramunas Navardauskas
Tom Peterson
Gabriel Rasch
Chris Anker Sörensen
Peter Stetina
Danny Summerhill
Andrew Talansky
Christian Vande Velde
Sep Vanmarcke
Johan Vansummeren
Matt Wilson
Dave Zabriskie

WOMEN'S TEAM

Noemi Cantele
Emma Pooley
Iris Slappendel

SLIPSTREAM SPORTS CEO AND SPORTING DIRECTOR

Jonathan Vaughters

SLIPSTREAM SPORTS OWNER

Doug Ellis

SLIPSTREAM SPORTS PRESIDENT

Matt Johnson

DIRECTEURS SPORTIFS

Bingen Fernandez
Lionel Marie
Eric van Lancker
Peter van Petegem
Johnny Weltz

TEAM MECHANICS

Alex Banyay
Geoff Brown
Eric Fostvedt
Joan Linares
Andrzej Pozak
Victor Villalba
Kris Withington

SPORTS SCIENCE DIRECTOR

Robby Ketchell

SOIGNEURS

Josep Colomer
Gavin King
Alyssa Morahan
John Murray
Sandra Ni Hodnae
Vincente Pana
Joachim Schoonaker

MEDICAL STAFF

Serge Niamke M.D.
Matt Rabin, M.Sc., D.C.
Kevin Reichlin, D.C.
Prentice Steffen, M.D.
Adrie van Diemen, M.D.

DIRECTOR OF COMMUNICATIONS

Marya Pongrace

DIRECTOR OF OPERATIONS

Louise Donald

MARKETING DIRECTOR

Alex Palmer

ATTORNEY

Matthew Pace

CHEFS

Olga Fowler
Sean Fowler
Barbara Grealish
Chris Grealish

BUS DRIVERS

Andrea Bisogno
Kevin Galos
Matthieu Rompion

Also mentioned in this text:

CERVÉLO

Tom Fowler
Gerard Vroomen
Phil White

GARMIN

Eric Bernard
Jon Cassat
Justin McCarthy
Caroline Murphy-Lassuie

MAVIC

François-Xavier Blanc

RACE ORGANIZERS

Serge Arsenault
Andrew Messick

UCI PRESIDENT

Pat McQuaid

WINTER TRAINING CAMP

Dave Zabriskie sits on a glowing Plexiglas stage in a darkened ballroom at the AC Hotel Palau de Bellavista, a hotel perched like a shimmering glass-and-steel sentry above the cobblestoned passageways of Girona. Dense curtains block views of the snowcapped Pyrenees. A lattice of studio lights illuminates the six-time U.S. time trial champion, while revolving fan blades cast shadows on a backdrop. A nest of Mavic wheels spins between the stage and boom-mounted television cameras. Zabriskie, the third American to wear the yellow jersey, following Greg LeMond and Lance Armstrong, looks like an action figure in a life-sized diorama.

DZ, as his teammates call him, stands up, puts his right hand on the small of his back, tilts slightly to the right, and winces. It's January 31 at the team's winter training camp, and while his Garmin-Cervélo teammates spent five hours riding in the Catalan countryside earlier today, back pain kept the 32-year-old off the bike. The American television network Versus is in Spain to film Zabriskie and his teammates talking about themselves. In four months the vignettes will be

broadcast during the Tour of California and then the Tour de France.

Script in hand, the director asks Zabriskie about sweltering days ahead in July. "The Tour de France; what is it that makes it such a special event?" Gliding on a dolly, the camera films Zabriskie's response. "The energy that everyone is feeling is different," he says. A machine suddenly pumps fog onto the set, and Zabriskie leaps up. The vegan waves his hands at a descending cloud. A camera operator assures him it is harmless. Zabriskie arches an eyebrow.

The assorted Garmin-Cervélo riders move through the three photo and video sets in the ballroom as if passing through stations of the cross. Christian Vande Velde, the U.S. star who has been with the team since 2008, rides the rollers for the camera.

When the director tells world champion Thor Hushovd they must be confusing him with stage directions, the Norwegian, a man of few words, responds with a faint smile. "I trust you guys."

While the veterans like Hushovd and Vande Velde take it all in stride—their work takes place on

ABOVE Dave Zabriskie on the television set in the team's hotel. RIGHT Rider decals before being applied to team bikes.

the road, but this is where the bills get paid—the younger riders, including 25-year-old Irishman Dan Martin, are agog. Martin, who turned pro with the team in 2008, snaps photos of the set with his camera phone.

※

THE DAY AFTER THE VERSUS FILMING WRAPS up, team director (*directeur sportif* in cycling vernacular) Bingen Fernandez sits in the soaring glass hotel lobby with his laptop open to a spreadsheet. It's a daunting digital abacus with hundreds of cells scheduling some 250 days of racing for the team's 29 riders over the next 10 months. Fernandez, 39, rode for six years with the Basque Euskaltel-Euskadi team and eight with French squad Cofidis. His experience is an asset for the still fairly young Garmin-Cervélo team.

The soft-spoken Basque says Garmin-Cervélo is different from traditional professional cycling teams. It takes an empirical approach to both winning races and creating a sustainable business that supports riders, staff, owners, and sponsors. "There must be a change in cycling," he says in Spanish. "I think we need to leave the old things in cycling behind and adapt ourselves to modern life." However, hailing from the tradition-bound Basque country, he also values his sport's conventions. "I like the old way of thinking a little bit," he says. "But I'm also inventive. I like a combination. I like to innovate on top, but preserve the roots."

Fernandez, who straddles worlds, cultures, and value systems, is a proxy for the revolutionary ethos of the Garmin-Cervélo team and how it is disrupting the 150-year-old profession's history. The team was started by ex-pro and current CEO and sporting director Jonathan Vaughters in 2003 as a development team for young U.S. riders. Vaughters is a one-time U.S. Postal Service rider who raced professionally from 1994 to 2004 in Europe and the United States, and a former teammate of U.S. superstar Lance Armstrong. Vaughters quit racing because he did not buy into a culture that systematically overlooked, hid, and ignored doping. Then he made it his goal to make the sport more financially stable for riders, team owners, sponsors, and race organizers. Slipstream, the holding company he created, is ushering in a new approach to the sport, most strikingly by rejecting drugs as tools for higher performance. Doping scandals scare sponsors away, and Vaughters knows that changing cycling's doping culture is key to ensuring the sport's financial stability.

The challenges inherent in this project are constant. The week before the camp kicks off, Vaughters fires the team's longtime directeur sportif Matt White, when he learns the Australian referred a past rider to a doctor not approved by the team. While it seems an honest mistake, the shadow of doubt is enough for Vaughters to can the well-liked and widely respected director, ending his three-year tenure.

Dan Martin says the move sends a valuable message to the organization at the beginning of the year. "It shows that there's no exceptions. Matt White is one of the most important parts of this team. He's crucial to the development of the team, and it shows that even he wasn't exempt from not playing by the rules."

In Martin's eyes, firing White keeps nonracing pressure off of the riders by making the team's success equation manifest: For any medical or nutritional issues, riders have doctors and scientists on hand whom they can trust. "We have to consult the team medical staff for everything. That takes the risk away from the team, and it takes the pressure off us as well," Martin says. The medical staff members, he adds, "have got our careers in their hands." There is neither a need nor an option to go outside this circle of vetted advisers. "I've grown up with this team, and it's the only way I've ever known.

"We've very much developed this anti-doping culture, as opposed to the sweep-it-under-the-rug culture," the talented young rider continues. "This transparency that we've had from the beginning is one of the reasons that I came to the team."

WHILE VAUGHTERS AND THE TEAM'S PRESS officer deal with the fallout of letting a longtime director go, across town it's just after sunrise at the team *service course*, when head mechanic Geoff Brown rolls up a metal door with a clatter that echoes across the frost-covered countryside. *Service course* is a cycling term for a team's mechanical headquarters, in this case a triple-bay garage in an industrial park on the outskirts of Girona. The unadorned cinder block structure swallows the team's bus and fleet of trucks and cars like a whale

On January 31, Christian Vande Velde (top) and Ryder Hesjedal film promotional pieces that will air during July's Tour de France.

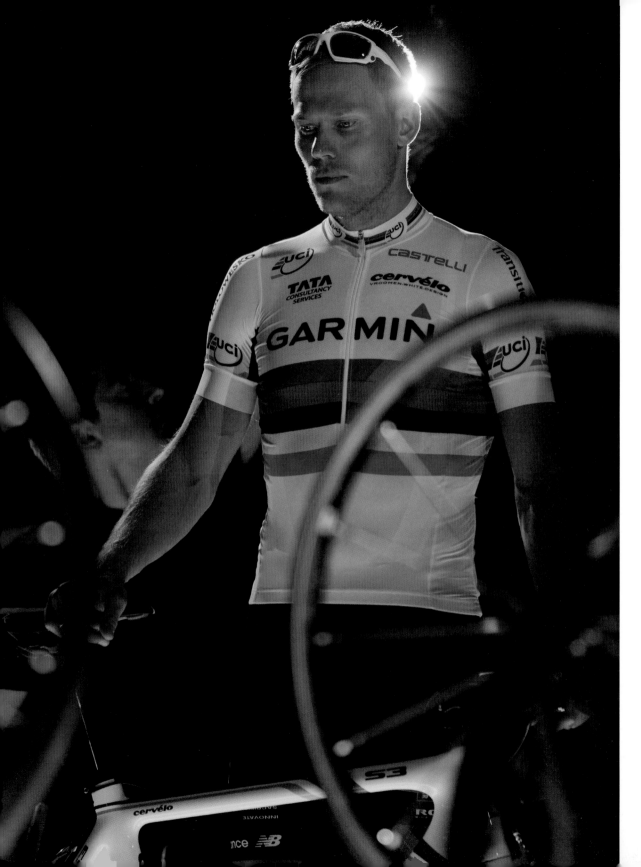

eating fish. The industrial park is so new the building does not yet have gas or electricity. Brown starts the morning by plugging a fat extension cord into a generator. Dressed in mechanic's overalls and a wool hat under a snugged sweatshirt hood, he pulls on a pair of gloves, walks to a well-used espresso machine, and brews a steaming cup of coffee.

Brown started working in his father's bike shop in Ottawa, Ontario, when he was a kid. After he wrenched for the Canadian national team through the 1992 Olympics, the Motorola team offered him a job that later became a position with the U.S. Postal team. "I headed off to Europe, and I've basically been here ever since," the 51-year-old says, laughing. He has seen a lot.

Next to Brown's bike stand, a recycling bin overflows with cardboard boxes from the hundreds of Cervélo bicycle frames and Mavic wheels that arrived during the previous week from the team's sponsors. Toward the back of the garage, a tower of unopened bike boxes awaits the arrival of the rest of the six-person mechanic staff.

ABOVE Andreas Klier trains indoors on a day dedicated to media interviews. LEFT Thor Hushovd in the rainbow-striped jersey he won at the 2010 World Championship road race in Australia.

The pretraining-camp tasks facing the mechanics during the last two weeks of January include assembling nearly 100 bikes, gluing tubular tires on some 300 carbon-fiber wheels, answering the riders' unique bike-fitting requests as they filter into town, and building up a fleet of bikes for sponsor VIPs who arrive on January 30—all while outfitting the garage's bare cinder block walls with racks and shelves to keep a season's worth of equipment in order. At the same time, the mechanics are packing wheels and bikes in a shipping container for transportation to the Middle East. There, the mechanics will assemble the equipment for February's Tours of Qatar and Oman.

By 8:30 the rest of the mechanics arrive. Spaniard Victor Villalba puts a Cervélo on a bike stand near the open door. Like an artisan stringing a guitar, he

LEFT Dressed for winter cold, head mechanic Geoff Brown builds bikes. BELOW In 2011 the team moved into a larger *service course*—a storage facility and mechanical shop—in a Girona industrial park. BOTTOM Brown reaches for one of the over $250,000 worth of Mavic wheels the mechanics will prepare during the course of the season.

TOP LEFT AND RIGHT Victor Villalba prepares bikes and tubular wheels for the racing season. BOTTOM Kris Withington coats a rim with tire adhesive.

pulls cables from a box and threads them through the top tube, his frozen breath illuminated by the early morning sun. With a small boom box next to him doing its best to fill the cavernous garage with European techno music, Villalba's work on the cables and bike assembly fills his morning.

After lunch at a nearby cafeteria, Villalba moves to a stepladder at a workbench, opens a red can of Italian mastic, and brushes the glue across the bottom of a partially inflated tire. His strokes are quick, precise, decisive. After one coat of glue, he tosses the tire to the floor; it looks like a truck crashed and lost its load of Hula Hoops at his feet.

Down the bench, New Zealander Kris Withington peers through horn-rimmed glasses at a wheel mounted on a truing stand. He slowly spins the $1,800 wheel—carbon-fiber from rim to spokes to hub—and brushes glue on its concave rim sur-

face. His work overalls have an AC/DC patch on one side of his chest and a New Zealand flag on the other; it would be easy to mistake the college-educated mechanic for a rock band roadie. Brown says that over the course of the season the squad glues 500 to 600 wheels. "I got strong fingers," he says. "And no brain cells. They've all been dissolved by the fumes!"

Completed wheels, already about 200 of them, hang on a rack at the back of the *service course*. At $140 per tire and $3,500 for each set of wheels, there is a reason the facility is secured by an alarm system and closed-circuit cameras. Behind the wheels, a separate shelf-lined room waits for the shipments of 20,000 CamelBak water bottles and 30,000 Clif Bars the team will use during the season.

Work on the wheels and bike building comes to a halt when a delivery truck pulls up with 140 boxes of North Face clothing and travel bags. Polish mechanic Andrzej Pozak and his Spanish colleague Joan Linares form a chain with Brown and soigneur Alyssa Morahan. A soigneur is a pro cycling jack-of-all-trades who does everything from massage therapy to preparing drink bottles to washing clothes to handing out bags in race feed zones. Without them and the mechanics, a pro cycling team would collapse. The group quickly unloads the truck into a tower of boxes in an adjoining service bay. Two days later, the garage will be lined with North Face suitcases, each one filled with North Face, Castelli, and New Balance clothing and shoes and tagged with the name of the rider and staff member or sponsor for distribution at the camp.

Riders begin filtering into the *service course* the following morning. It's their private bike shop, where any problem can be solved at no cost to them. Colorado native Peter Stetina, 24, arrives on his bike with a time trial frame over his shoulder. The following week, after camp is under way, Matt Wilson shows up a couple of hours before a scheduled 10 a.m. training ride. The 34-year-old Australian national champion is fresh off a plane from the Tour Down Under race in his homeland. "I think this frame is too big," he tells Pozak.

The quiet Polish mechanic pulls a 56-centimeter Cervélo S3 from a shipping box and puts it on a stand. Then he places Wilson's 58-centimeter bike on a jig that measures bicycle dimensions and carefully records its every facet, down to the millimeter: seat to handlebar, top of seat to bottom bracket, seat setback from bottom bracket. Dressed in riding tights and booties, Wilson crosses his arms against the cold air. Pozak switches all the components

LEFT Soigneur Alyssa Morahan unloads boxes of gear at the *service course*. BELOW Luggage before distribution at the winter training camp. The scooter is for motorpacing.

ABOVE Matt Wilson watches as mechanic Andrzej Pozak switches Wilson from a 58- to a 56-cm frame. BELOW Christian Vande Velde with wife, Leah, and daughters at the *service course*.

from one frame to another, while the Australian watches carefully, only occasionally asking questions about the setup. Wilson interacts with the skilled mechanic with the gravity of a patient consulting his surgeon.

Two sponsors from Rotor, the team's Spanish crankset supplier show up. One of them takes off his orange down vest and offers it to Wilson. The Australian gratefully puts it on. Thirty minutes later, the frames are swapped and Wilson takes the new bike for a spin around the garage.

Suddenly, the garage is awash with riders and people affiliated with the teams' various sponsors. The day is to start with sponsors riding with the team through the bucolic Catalan landscape. The mechanics rush to adjust seat heights on the fleet of Cervélos they just finished building for the VIPs.

Outside, Hushovd pedals over to Jon Cassat, Garmin's vice president of communications and a keen cyclist in his own right. Hushovd shows his Garmin Edge GPS unit to Cassat. Heads bent together over the device, they converse like kids studying a butterfly. This camp is one of the few times Cassat can build a relationship with riders outside of the races, where they are preoccupied. "We're going to download new software to his Edge," Cassat says later. Referring to the bonds that form over their common passion for cycling, the vice president explains, "I couldn't do that if I wasn't building a relationship with Thor Hushovd and riding with him on a Sunday morning. I don't know how you put a value on that kind of thing, but that is why we are here."

Cassat, who has been with Garmin since 1993, says the company first sponsored the team in 2008 for business reasons. "We didn't do this for the love of cycling, and we still don't justify it based on the love of cycling." Garmin's involvement with the team is a split from cycling's past, where traditionally a wealthy cycling enthusiast who also happened to be a European industrialist would single-handedly bankroll and manage a team. "Our CEO doesn't ride, our president doesn't ride," says Cassat. "This is about reaching a fan base that represents a customer base for us."

"The guys are riding their asses off," Cassat says. "They take it pretty seriously. I think the low point to the riders is having to have dinner and drinks with the sponsors! My hope is that when I walk in the room they don't think, 'Oh, there's that asshole sponsor that I gotta to be nice to.'"

THE TEAM, BOTH THE MEN'S AND WOMEN'S squads, are putting in serious saddle time indeed— about six hours a day. On the second day of camp at 10 a.m. the squads pour into the *service course* from the hotel and their Girona homes and apartments. Without clipping out of their pedals, they ride to a table the soigneurs have set up at the back of the garage and go locust on the waiting Clif Bars, bananas, and water bottles. Andreas Klier and Roger Hammond, elder statesmen at 35 and 37, joke about the cold that leaves their breath hanging in air.

Directors Lionel Marie and Johnny Weltz map out a 100-mile loop that starts by taking the riders over Els Angles, a local climb that tops out at a whitewashed monastery where Salvador Dalí and his second wife, Gala, married in 1958. Except for a

LEFT Loading up with fluids and food before a six-hour training ride. BELOW Riders listen to instructions before breaking into smaller groups for a team time trial workout.

handful of riders racing in Australia, the full squads are here, an occurrence that will not happen again during the racing season. On the way up the twisting, 6-mile, 1,588-foot ascent, Martin taps out a steady cadence at the front, while Noemi Cantele from the women's team rides comfortably behind him. At the top, a few riders strip off their Castelli wind jackets and get more food from the car. Single file over the top, they sibilate down the climb like a blue and black snake beneath a canopy of oak trees. The roads are astonishingly scenic and free of cars. You can understand why Weltz, a Dane who rode for the Spanish ONCE squad, settled here with his family more than two decades ago.

Johan Vansummeren flats as the team enters a series of rolling hills. For these guys, there are no tire irons and finicky frame pumps. The 6-foot, 5-inch Belgian calmly steps off his bike, removes his front wheel, and hands it to Weltz, who appears with a replacement. The rest of the riders do not wait, and Vansummeren does a monster interval over the undulating terrain to catch them.

The group stops to pee four times throughout the day. As if through occult communication, they just suddenly pull over en masse and water the landscape. During the third stop, in the woods at the bottom of a slashing climb, the riders mash into the back of Weltz's support car, pulling bottles from a stocked cooler and tossing old bottles back. The tidy station wagon becomes a chaos of bottles, jackets, and Clif Bar wrappers.

In the cold, legs get stiff. British rider David Millar growls, "Let's go. We aren't out here to stand around." As quickly as they stopped, the riders stream up the next hill as lightly as 30 blue fireflies.

OPPOSITE Riders form an echelon while going through a team time trial exercise in Catalonia, Spain. ABOVE Five hours into a ride, smoke rises from a farmhouse as the team heads back to Girona.

RIGHT Dan Martin and Tom Peterson take a pull during a February 1 training ride. OPPOSITE January 29 team presentation in Girona's AC Hotel Palau de Bellavista.

After a couple of hours, Weltz stops his car, flags down the riders, and breaks the team into five-rider groups. Turning onto a highway with a wide shoulder, Millar, Wilson, American Tyler Farrar, Vande Velde, and Australian Brett Lancaster form a pace line. When he gets to the front of the line, 31-year-old Lancaster melts off to the left. Like a suitcase landing on an airport conveyer belt, he drifts to the back, where 10 brisk standing pedal strokes push him into the low-pressure zone behind Farrar's rear wheel. Hands draped casually over his shifters, Millar neither flinches nor accelerates when Lancaster exposes him to the gutting head wind. Set to the whir of chain over sprockets and the occasional chunk of a gear shift, it's a glorious flow; notes on a score. After two 10-minute intervals,

Weltz waves the riders down. Their faces glisten with sweat in the 38-degree windchill.

THAT NIGHT, THE RIDERS FILTER INTO THE AC Palau lobby at 7:00. Gathered sponsors and VIPs pluck champagne and tapas from trays carried by a stream of waiters. One important person who could not make the trip to Girona is the team's owner and generous financial backer, Doug Ellis. In 2005, Ellis, a longtime cycling fan, was intrigued by the U.S. development team Vaughters started in 2003. The 47-year-old businessman cold-called the racing director and asked how he could get involved. The team was about to introduce its TIAA-CREF squad at a Denver restaurant. "Jonathan said the dinner was sold out, but if I could get to Denver, he would sneak me in through the kitchen," Ellis recalls of their first meeting in 2005. He flew to Colorado, was impressed by what he saw, and that led to Ellis offering financial and moral encouragement for Vaughters to expand his sights to international-level pro cycling.

In 2007, Ellis, who grew up near Boston and now lives and manages his business interests from New York City, provided funding that allowed Vaughters to hire riders like Vande Velde and Millar for the 2008 season, a squad with enough firepower to earn the team an invite to that year's Tour de France, where Vande Velde placed fourth. As for what inspired him to make that first call to Vaughters and then back it up with millions of dollars, Ellis says, "It was just a love of the sport." Ellis is a private investor; he has no public company to publicize through the team. Refined, yet down to earth, he speaks with a soft, even-tempered calmness that's void of bluster and the stereotypical New York businessman's hard-edged pushiness. Without a trace of pretension, he states that his designs were no more complicated than joining Vaughters to help ease talented Americans into cycling's European culture. His initial phone call was motivated by "some instinct that we could build a platform to get more U.S. athletes into the sport." While a U.S. rider might have the physical talent to make it in Europe, just dropping him into a team in Italy might not work, Ellis explains. "He might be totally competent athletically and fail for cultural reasons." He adds, "You can't hold these guys' hands for years and years, but is there a way we can make a program that just helps

World time trial champion Emma Pooley at the team presentation party.

them develop some ability to last longer before they move on? That's really what our program was like in the beginning years—we actually had dormitories in Girona." Thinking back to 2005, he reflects, "I really didn't have any kind of expectation about what it was going to be like. In fact I really wasn't even thinking about the business. I was really just thinking about the sport."

TONIGHT, SIX YEARS AFTER THAT FATEFUL dinner in Denver, Vaughters and American television cycling commentator Robbie Ventura stride

onto a balcony overlooking the lobby. Ventura invites riders up in groups. The first includes Zabriskie, Wilson, Vande Velde, Vansummeren, and Belgian Sep Vanmarcke. Ventura turns to Vaughters, "Tell us about Sep Vanmarcke."

With obvious pride, Vaughters points out that as a 20-year-old in 2010, "Sep was second place at Ghent-Wevelgem," the 136-mile Belgian semi-classic race. "He is just an immense talent and a really, really humble and great person. Physically, the kid's incredible."

When women's team rider and world time trial champion Emma Pooley comes up, Vaughters mentions that in addition to landing a world championship title, the Englishwoman is a PhD candidate. Taking a wireless microphone, Pooley shyly explains that her graduate studies have been forced into a secondary position. "I'm a professional cyclist now."

"You heard it here first," Vaughters adds to the crowd's delight; "'My PhD is like a hobby.'"

The following day is a Sunday. After a 120-mile morning ride, 15 riders gather around a laptop in the hotel lobby. The computer is streaming the cyclocross world championships from Germany. When a French rider bumps another cyclocrosser, Aussie-German Heinrich Haussler groans, "Ahh, Froggy!" Six-time British cyclocross national champion Roger Hammond glances over his shoulder and smiles at Frenchman Christophe Le Mével behind him. Clad in matching black tracksuits with big Cervélo é logos on the back, the riders look like free-spirited schoolboys.

Hushovd sits in a separate corner of the lobby, bathed in soft light that pours in from the high windows, tapping away on his laptop. When eventual

race winner Zdenek Stybar attacks with Sven Nys, the cluster of Garmin-Cervélo men let out a roar. Smiling, Hushovd walks over and peers at the computer screen from behind the group.

On the other side of the lobby and hidden behind the bar, Vaughters, team president Matt Johnson, and operations director Louise Donald are also huddling over laptops. Rather than watching cyclocross, however, they pore over spreadsheets to figure out how to make the team's finances last through the year. With a budget that is about 30 percent of most well-financed ProTour teams (and ninth out of the top 18 ProTour teams), Vaughters, Johnson, and Donald have to make hard decisions about where to spend their money. Does the team buy a new bus or keep milking the old one along, which they bought used from another team? On top of the expense of flying 29 athletes all over the world, sometimes paying last-minute airfares, there are budgetary decisions such as whether to replace the team's 12 Skoda automobiles—cars that are used extremely hard, not just during races, but also during the monumental transfers between countries all over Europe.

The team watches a live Internet feed of the cyclocross world championships in Germany.

To keep it all going, Johnson is constantly selling. Working with a designer, a writer, and a pool of photographers, he prepares and sends out some 40 sponsor pitches each year in a grinding effort to feed the financial beast that is a pro team race schedule.

A TRAINING RIDE TWO DAYS LATER TAKES the team from Girona southeast to the Mediterranean Sea. On the way out, Tyler Farrar's seatpost slips, and his seat inches down. The team bikes are brand-new, and training camp is where kinks like these are worked out before the real racing starts. Weltz pulls over the follow car and tightens the seat bolt. Minutes later the seatpost slips again, and Weltz repeats the process. Then, while Farrar hammers down a narrow farm road across a muddy, furrowed field, the sprinter from Washington State stops a third time. Even from 100 yards away, his tense body language speaks fury. He grabs his bike by the seat and top tube, winds up like a discus-thrower, and hurls it into the field.

"We'll go back to the *service course* and get another bike," Weltz tells Farrar when we pull up. Fuming, Farrar gets in the front seat, while Weltz puts the muddy bike on the roof rack. On the way back Farrar wonders aloud. "Why the fuck is there grease on the seatpost?" He is sorely disappointed by the interruption to a day of hard training.

Weltz pats Farrar's leg. "You can motorpace back to the coast." He points to the sun above the mountains to the east. "It will be warm in the afternoon." Farrar's mood brightens in the 49-year-old direc-

LEFT Peter Stetina rides near the summit of Els Angles, a regular train-ing climb above Girona. BELOW Tyler Farrar hitches a ride up from the Mediterranean Sea near Tossa del Mar. OPPOSITE CEO Jonathan Vaughters discusses the team's budget with president Matt Johnson and operations director Louise Donald.

tor's calm presence. He looks at Weltz and smiles, plainly savoring the prospect of an unexpected hour of motorpacing on Girona's empty roads.

Weltz drives while wielding a cell phone in each hand. At the *service course* Joan Linares waits out front with a bike. Although the mechanics are bur-ied with work, Brown tells Linares to get in the car in case the seatpost starts misbehaving again—Australian national champion Travis Meyer is hav-ing the same problem. Before the riders return, all the mechanics get an e-mail from Brown with a heads-up about the slipping posts so the problem won't happen again.

As the station wagon heads back out toward the coast, its speedometer sits unwaveringly at 65 kmh

(40 mph). From inside the car, Farrar looks like a fish swimming in a tank, his face inches from the rear window. He is hardly breathing. We get to the coastal resort of Tossa del Mar then turn inland again on a long, twisting climb away from the ocean. We still haven't caught the team; Farrar grabs the top of the car as Weltz tows him up the steeper sections to the 1,181-foot-high stone hermitage of Sant Grau, a wooded sanctuary that dates back to the fifteenth century. Farrar leans into the passenger window: "I'm glad we got some motorpacing in. I needed that."

He catches the rest of the team just beneath the hermitage. About a mile into the team's corkscrew-ing descent, the riders skid to a stop on the under-side of a sharp bend where Farrar has crashed.

Farrar stands in the middle of the crowd, arm bleeding, jersey torn, a hole in his shorts. Weltz jumps from the car and looks carefully into Farrar's eyes.

"I think I hit some sand," Farrar tells him.

While Linares inspects Farrar's bike and adjusts his brakes, Weltz quizzes Farrar. "You OK, Tyler? Do you want to get in the car?" He doesn't. Satisfied that Farrar has not knocked himself in the head or broken anything, Weltz gives him the go-ahead to ride. In the car, Weltz says, "It's a tense day; I could tell from the start."

·These guys ride hard, and sponsors such as Mavic like that. The French component maker's François-Xavier Blanc is at the camp to collect feedback from the riders and mechanics. He says the team's exceptional use can reveal weaknesses in a product. "The way a regular consumer is using our products and the way those guys are using the products is different," Blanc explains. And that uncovers issues Mavic might never see with products sold to the public. For instance, when in the middle of a peloton of 200 riders traveling at 40 mph, pros hit rocks and potholes at a regularity and velocity that does not happen anywhere else. "Sometimes we discover issues that we don't see during our testing process," Blanc adds.

While the riders and mechanics put a lot of trust in Mavic's wheels, the company in turn has faith in Vaughters's project. "We trust this team, we trust Jonathan, we trust what he is doing," Blanc tells me. Without a hint of PR gloss, Blanc adds that Mavic sees Vaughters's anti-doping culture and drive to make the sport more economically stable as "the future of cycling." Blanc likes the new forces entering the sport with more catholic, empirical

approaches. "Today smart guys like Jonathan are kicking the ass of the former Italians and Belgians. For me, it's a revolution."

A few hours after Farrar wipes out, the riders pull in to an industrial area outside the town of La Bisbal d'Empordà. Meters past a store with a yard full of ceramic pots and statues and across an empty field from a Cespa-Elf fuel station, they do a lap through a roundabout. They are looking for something; this is the sort of location only cyclists who spend their days seeking out-of-the-way places might find. The riders pour into a driveway and get off their bikes in front of Bar & Restaurant El Ranxo (El Ranxo means "the ranch" in Catalan).

One after another, they stack roughly half-a-million-dollars' worth of bicycles in front of the café, which is improbably located in an industrial building next to the Zero Zero Grow Shop. Tom Danielson, born in Connecticut but now a Colorado resident, pushes open a pair of Old West–style doors, above which is a cartoon figure of a smiling green horse. The animal wears a red bib and holds a knife and fork in its hooves. The riders fill the café with the clop of cleats on hardwood. Cyclists are common in Catalonia; few customers take notice.

Farrar, Danielson, and Haussler pull up stools to the bar and order. *"Café con leche, por favor."* Farrar's left shoulder is still blackened with road grime, but he seems unfazed. Brazilian national champion Murilo Fischer sits at a table and laughs with Lithuanian national champ Ramunas Navardauskas; these are two of the most gracious guys on the squad, and their good humor masks the pair's fearsome capacity to rip the legs off of mortals. After coffee and pastries inside, Hushovd, Klier,

OPPOSITE Coffee time at the El Ranxo bar and restaurant.

19

TOP Peter Stetina arrives at the *service course* with a time trial frame carried from his apartment in Girona. BOTTOM A bike packing list in the *service course* for February's Tours of Oman and Qatar.

and Hammond wander outside and slouch on red plastic molded chairs in the parking lot. Haussler joins them. Klier and Hushovd poke and pull at the straps on their Giro helmets, dialing in the fit.

Later Hammond, a 37-year-old British classics specialist who came over from the Cervélo team that Garmin merged with at the end of 2010, says he really enjoys this preseason chance to ride with the entire squad. At races, riders fly in the day before, see each other in the evening, and "it's high stress from there on," Hammond observes. He is low-key, but he knows pressure. The multitime British national road and cyclocross champion has placed third and fourth at the monumental French one-day Paris-Roubaix race and second at the Belgian semi-classic Ghent-Wevelgem. While the tension might not be apparent to an onlooker, Hammond says racing "is quite a heavy situation" that can profoundly alter a rider's character. In contrast, on these days in Girona, "You've got hours to pass the time together, get to know each other, and build good relationships, because people are very, very different without stress." Even though the team might be riding six hours at a steady 25 mph tempo, for Hammond, tempo makes all the difference. "You come here and do the big miles with the team, sit in the center for quite some time, and just ride."

The next day it rains. The riders are scheduled to do a short ride in the morning then return to the hotel for media interviews. It's not just wet outside; it's cold. The directors call off the ride, and the entire day is now dedicated to media interviews and time riding trainers set up in a hotel function room. Everyone gets the memo except for Canadian Ryder Hesjedal, seventh in the 2010 Tour de France, who

walks into the hotel lobby soaking wet in his rain gear and booties. The lobby fills with journalists and photographers. Two or three are always waiting to talk to Hushovd. The team's communications director, Marya Pongrace, gently taps reporters on the shoulder when their time with Hushovd is done.

I sit down with Vaughters in the lobby. "When you are 80, what do you want Jonathan Vaughters's legacy to be?" I ask.

Vaughters, 38, lets out a short bark of a laugh, "Huh!" It's a sound akin to improperly toed brake shoes on a bike rim. He does this a lot. It's as if a proposition plops into his mind like a stone in a pond: If your idea is stupid, the sound represents spreading waves of dismissal. If it's profound, it marks appreciation. The "huh!" sounds the same for both circumstances, so you never really know where you stand with Vaughters. "My dream would be, yeah, that I would be the guy that people point to and say, okay, he started the profound change in cycling. And not just anti-doping, but that it becomes a more professional, more transparent, more consumer-friendly, more stable and healthy place for the athletes to be. Across the board, a more cooperative sport."

The fact that the entire team will be together only once this year, here at this camp, unlike other sports where players unify every week for practices and games, is symbolic of the sport's fundamentally scattered and primitive nature. It's a fractured state that Vaughters has made it his personal and professional mission to change, both by creating this team and by taking on the leadership of the AIGCP (Association International des Groupes Cyclistes Professionels), an organization that represents teams and their owners. "There is no long-term strategic vision for the global aspect of the sport," he observes. "It just doesn't exist. Everyone's doing their own thing."

Vaughters compares the current state of professional cycling to wind tunnel testing on a bicycle wheel, but not factoring in the effects of the frame, components, and rider. "It's the interaction of the whole" that is not being considered, he says. When I ask him what would motivate cycling's various stakeholders—riders, team owners, race organizers—to take a long-term, holistic approach, he says, "Definitive evidence that they would eventually benefit from the whole being much bigger."

As his Basque director points out, Vaughters is, above all, an empiricist. He knows the danger in dogmatism; his data are incomplete, and everything is subject to revision. "There has to be some real empirical evidence for people to make that leap of faith," he says. "And even if there were, I think it would be viewed with suspicion."

Vaughters has a roving mind; he has written for the *Wine Spectator* and is always conversant in the contents of the latest *New Yorker*. He is a student of sport, economy, and culture. As an American trying to change a European sport, he is aware that his upbringing equips him with a New World bias that both enables and hobbles his project. He points out that American sports like baseball and football were also fractured at various points in their history. What makes pro cycling different is that it rests on a different set of commercial assumptions than the ones underpinning those sports. "In America, everything always reverts to its mean, because you've got a constant entrepreneurial push. It is just

ABOVE Delayed by mechanical difficulties, Tyler Farrar catches up with his fellow riders by motor-pacing behind a team car at 40 mph. LEFT Martijn Maaskant and Tyler Farrar relax in the team hotel after training.

what the society is." In his home country, Vaughters maintains, fractured interests in sports like baseball and football always come back together, unified by the glue of making more money. "In Europe," Vaughters says, with a mix of admiration and frustration, "personal differences are not given up over something as silly as money."

Looking out from the vantage point of February and another year ahead tilting at the unruly sport that defines his life, Vaughters cautions that there is no way he can be the person that reforms pro cycling. The hard work of change is done by a host of unheralded experts, anti-doping scientists, business people, and athletes. Fifty years on from this gray morning in a city with two millennia of human transactions under its skin, he says he would like to look back and see himself as a spur: "the one that basically kept throwing the arguments out there and was known as the catalyst that fundamentally reformed the sport of cycling into something a whole lot better than it used to be. Yeah, that would be great."

THE COBBLED CLASSICS

TOUR OF FLANDERS AND PARIS-ROUBAIX

Two days before the Tour of Flanders, Matt Wilson, Daniel Lloyd, Andreas Klier, Thor Hushovd, Johan Vansummeren, and Heinrich Haussler roll out from the Hotel Lepelbed for an easy spin in the Belgian countryside. Six miles outside the medieval city of Ghent, the Lepelbed is a snug 19-room place with framed cycling jerseys on the walls. It feels more like a big house than a hotel. And that's why it's the team's base the first few weeks of the Spring Classics, a one-month stretch of prestigious one-day races in Belgium, Holland, and France that starts with Ghent-Wevelgem the last weekend in March and ends with mountainous Liège-Bastogne-Liège the final weekend in April.

The Tour of Flanders, or Ronde van Vlaanderen, as it's called in Flemish, dates back to 1913 and is the most important race in Belgium. The 160-mile course connects 18 hills, *hellingen*, that are paved with bone-jarring cobbles.

With a start that drops due south from Bruges then cuts a snarled, backtracking path east to the finish in Ninove, the course map looks like a six-year-old's map of the constellations—one that starts with an earnest attempt at a skyward-thrusting scorpion tail then devolves into a scribbling line by the time the pencil gets to the body. Each climb is a luminary in Belgian cycling history, and all are heavily populated on race day with raging parties of *frites*-eating, beer-drinking cycling nuts. While the Tour de France attracts a huge volume of fans, there is nothing comparable to the DNA-deep ardor of the followers of the Ronde.

Haussler knows this love; he placed second in 2010, with Hammond five places back in seventh. Klier came close in 2005, finishing second between winner Tom Boonen and third-place Peter van Petegem. With the dismissal of Matt White, the team has hired Van Petegem, now a retired two-time Ronde and one-time Roubaix winner, to direct the riders at the cobbled classics, the cobblestone-heavy events in the first half of the Spring Classics month.

Media coverage is hyping the fact that with Van Petegem at the helm and such a stacked list of experienced riders, Garmin-Cervèlo is the team to neutralize Swiss powerhouse Fabian Cancellara, who demolished all comers at both Flanders and

Paris-Roubaix in 2010. The team's prospects seem to have put Hushovd in good spirits. As the riders ride side by side down the bike path in front of the Lepelbed, he whistles a tune.

After a half hour of riding through green fields and sleepy villages of tidy brick houses, the riders pile into Taverne Evora, a café in the small farm town of Oosterzele. They stack their bikes against a flower-topped patio wall and clatter inside. Hushovd unzips his vest and sits at a table. Klier has lived in Belgium since 1999. He orders coffees and sugared crêpes—savory Belgian *pannekoeken*—in fluent Flemish. Helping his mother prepare the coffees at the bar, a wide-eyed 13-year-old boy whispers to her, "That's Thor Hushovd."

Haussler's phone rings. It's Van Petegem looking for the café address. In Belgium, cycling is religion, and when the dark-skinned director walks through the door a few minutes later, it's like Jesus showing up at a party where Moses and the disciples are already rocking. The boy's grandfather disappears and comes back with a camera. The boy poses for photos with Van Petegem, who gracefully obliges the grandfather's wish for a shot of his grandson with a Belgian sporting god. He also gets a photo of the boy with Hushovd, and may later come to regret not getting one with Vansummeren, who slouches in his chair, cleans his glasses, fiddles with his helmet, and peers into an adjoining room decorated with black and white photographs of exhausted, rain-soaked racing cyclists.

The riders order a second round of coffees, exchange knowing glances as they discuss which other teams' riders are on special form for Sunday, chat about cell phone plans and the chance of rain.

ABOVE On the Friday before the Tour of Flanders, Thor Hushovd whistles past a storefront near Ghent, Belgium. RIGHT A local rider finds himself sharing a bike path with Andreas Klier, Dan Lloyd (obscured), Thor Hushovd, Heinrich Haussler, and Johan Vansummeren.

After an hour, they collect their clothes, phones, and helmets and step outside. The boy wheels his road bike out and shyly shows it to Haussler. His grandfather stands behind, proudly rubbing his grandson's shoulders.

AT THE LEPELBED, KLIER ASKS WILSON HOW long they rode. The Australian pokes a button on his Garmin. "One hour, one minute." In dead-pan English with a clipped German accent, Klier replies, "One minute too long. But that's okay." They leave their bikes with mechanic Kris Withington. After the bikes are scrubbed with soap and water, Withington puts Wilson's bike on a stand, lubes the chain, and checks the drivetrain and wheels for adjustments. The process happens every time the riders get off their bikes. I ask the Kiwi if he ever gets a weekend off, and he gives me a dismissive laugh. "Not since January."

That night, Klier, who started racing profes-sionally in 1996, already seems defeated by Cancellara. "Even if a group of guys goes with him and they had 10 legs each, they could not beat his two." And if Klier himself gets away with Cancellara and the Swiss champion asks Klier to pull through? Klier gives a ponderous shake of his head. He will decline. "I will just say, 'I am 35 years old.'"

The process of selecting riders for a race like Flanders involves assembling both intellectual and physical assets. Wisdom—classics racing experience plus time—is the cerebral materiel Klier brings to the team. It is a quality that compensates for the aging processes that now make it difficult for him to

play a closing role in these 160-mile races. "Without Andreas, the classics team just can't work," Vaughters notes. "He has great observational powers; he's good at using his experience to predict what's going to happen and dictate the tactics based on that." Most importantly, Klier knits the points of view of younger, rawer talents like Haussler and Farrar into a whole. Like a coxswain on a crew team, he unifies forces. "Tyler Farrar sees the race from Tyler Farrar's perspective," Vaughters notes. "Andreas Klier sees the race from the global perspective."

That global insight comes into play long before the riders roll out of Bruges's spectacular Market Square on race morning. Two nights before the race, Klier, Louise Donald, and Joachim Schoonaker pore over maps of the Flanders route. Schoonaker, a 30-year-old soigneur, comes from a family of Belgian cyclists. Five team support cars will be on the road at Flanders, one in the race caravan and four hopscotching to predetermined locations, where they'll wait with wheels and water. Donald and Schoonaker are preparing a set of maps for each car. "It's the wrong direction," Klier tells Schoonaker as they discuss how to get a car away from a climb. The German's encyclopedic knowl-edge of Belgian roads and pathways has earned him the nickname "GPS Klier." At the top of the day's sixth climb, the Knokteberg, written instructions on the map say, "Park car on Ronde van Vlaanderen Straat 300 meters from climb, so you can exit for Eikenberg." Driving directions are highlighted in green, with blue arrows indicating which direction to go. Parking areas are in pink.

Race organizers have issued the team only three sets of race vehicle stickers. That's a problem,

At the Hotel Lepelbed in Melle, Belgium, mechanics prepare bikes for the cobbled classics.

because the cars will need to travel on the course to get from one section to another. Donald looks at Van Petegem sitting in a leather chair in front of the fireplace. "I'll see what I can do." He punches a number into his cell phone.

A few minutes later, Van Petegem lifts two fingers. "Oh good, we got two more," Donald announces. Vaughters enters the room, glances at Van Petegem, and says, "We are winning, right?" The director, who will ride in the passenger seat while Vaughters drives, nods.

The night before the Ronde, Vaughters holds a briefing with the riders. Daniel Benson, a journalist from the CyclingNews Web site, sits in on the meeting. Vaughters reminds the riders that

tomorrow's radio communications between team cars and riders will be on TV. It's a broadcast deal Vaughters helped broker between the teams and the race organizer, Flanders Classics. In the future, teams could potentially license to race broadcasters the right to broadcast from inside race vehicles. After all, the inside-the-race discussions that go on in the team cars is extremely interesting to viewers, which gives this content value that cash-strapped teams could capitalize on and broadcasters could use to add depth to TV coverage. The innovation, old news in auto racing but new to cycling, is also a response to the ongoing efforts by the sport's governing body, the Union Cycliste Internationale, or UCI, to kill off radio communications between managers and riders. Ostensibly, this is because French television complains that race radios make racing too predictable.

Both Klier and Van Petegem describe the critical points in the race. Klier even details the angle of approach for certain turns. Because the peloton jams up on the steeper climbs, Van Petegem says the support staff should be waiting at the top of the climbs with extra shoes; cleats can break when riders get off and run.

But as the meeting wraps up, things turn sour. The riders discover Benson has been filming with his digital camera. They don't like not being told beforehand. Farrar is fuming. Vaughters pulls Benson into another room and asks him not to put the meeting online, out of respect for the riders' wishes.

Later Vaughters admits that it was his fault for not telling the riders Benson would be recording. It's not that video cameras are a problem. After all, a crew filming a *Beyond the Peloton* video series for

Halfway into an hour spin, riders take their coffee at the Taverne Evora in Oosterzele, Belgium.

Cervélo has also taped the meeting. But while the riders are accustomed to having the *Beyond the Peloton* crew constantly recording intimate moments, those films don't see the light of day for months. CyclingNews coverage, on the other hand, could end up online in hours, tipping off other teams to Garmin-Cervélo's pre-race strategy. Most significantly, the riders do not like being caught off guard.

Vaughters doesn't think Benson's recording is an issue; the team has nothing to hide. But Vaughters and his staff are responsible for providing a predictable environment for the athletes, and on these grounds, he failed. "Most people have to deal with a certain amount of chaos in their lives, but riders don't like chaos. They can't handle it," he says. In the nonjudgmental tone of an ex-pro who knows where his riders' heads are, he continues, "The race is chaotic enough. As soon as they step off the bike, they want everything to be very plain vanilla, and if it's not, it's really upsetting."

IN BELGIUM, THE TOUR OF FLANDERS carries the significance of Super Bowl Sunday in the United States or a World Cup final anywhere else; it immobilizes the nation. The riders know this, and at their 6:30 breakfast on race morning, their faces show the pressure is on. After their failure to deliver a win at the first Monument of the

Before sunrise has begun to illuminate the windows of the Hotel Lepelbed, classics director Peter van Petegem reads the sporting news on the morning of the Ronde van Vlaanderen, a race he won in 1999 and 2003.

year, March's Milan–San Remo, followed by Farrar's deflating third place at Ghent-Wevelgem, the team needs results. While Klier manages a quick laugh over his coffee, even the usually goofing Haussler is poker-faced as the riders dig into muesli, crêpes, bread, jam, and Nutella. Hushovd pads into the room, grabs two slices of ham from the breakfast buffet, carefully places them on a slice of bread, and returns to the team table to sit and eat in silence.

Van Petegem flips through a Ghent newspaper that includes 36 pages of Ronde coverage and a color front-page photo of Belgian cycling superstar Tom Boonen. At 7:00, Matt Johnson, Louise Donald, and marketing director Alex Palmer drive to a hotel to pick up guests from Tata, an Indian technology consulting firm and team sponsor. Tata's marketing director waits in the parking lot. The Frenchman is excited. He is accustomed to taking clients to Formula One auto races. "This is more interactive," he says of pro cycling. At F1 by comparison, "there are rules for everything, and nothing can change at the last moment." About 15 Tata managers and important clients chat over coffee and pastries in the hotel bar. Donald announces the day's agenda: After watching the riders sign in for the race in Bruges, vans will take the VIPs to several viewing spots along the course. They will make a stop for Belgian *frites* and beer, then head to the finish. Palmer distributes goodie bags containing hats and T-shirts. The guests' eyes shine with delight.

Close to the race start, a pack of guys is already drinking beer in the underground parking lot beneath Bruges's stunning, ornate Market Square. Above, fans are thick for kilometers along the race route as it snakes out of town.

A BREAK FORMS SOME 30 MILES INTO the race, and Hammond is in it. On the Knokteberg, the sixth climb of the day and 102 miles into the race, a family has a spread of food set up in front of their house and a keg of rich Belgian beer tapped in the driveway. Up the road, more fans wave Flanders flags like yellow and black butterflies in the soft

At the start of the 95th running of the Ronde van Vlaanderen, Thor Hushovd meets his fans in Bruges's 2,000-year-old Market Square.

spring sunshine. Hammond's eyes are welded to the wheel in front of him; he doesn't give Johnson, who is waiting with wheels and water at the top of the hill, a glance. Five or so minutes later, the field passes through, with the Garmin-Cervélo riders following Lloyd in a single-file formation that attests to the chase's rattling speed.

The field eventually catches Hammond at the top of the crowded, 22 percent grade of the Koppenberg, where a cardboard sign attached to a street mirror directs thousands of beer-happy fans toward a WC. It's 120 miles into the race, and Hushovd sits comfortably at the front. Behind him, gaps appear in the disintegrating field. Just before the 14th climb of the day, the Leberg, Hushovd unleashes a withering attack, but two-time Ronde winner Boonen counters and rides away in pursuit of Frenchman Sylvain Chavanel of the Quick-Step team. At the top of the Leberg, Cancellara attacks the field in front of an inflating hot air balloon, and the world time trial champion is gone. Seconds later, Haussler and Hushovd follow in a group containing American veteran George Hincapie, riding for BMC, and Farrar. The television broadcast patches into the Garmin-Cervélo radio feed in time to hear Vaughters announce: "Tyler, Thor, no riding, no riding!"

In bike-racing parlance, *no riding* means sit in the peloton; don't burn energy forcing the pace at the front. Instructing his two strongest sprinters not to work puts the onus on other teams to bring back Cancellara. That gamble proves right, as an attacking splinter group catches Cancellara 10 miles from the finish line. But that splinter does not include Hushovd and Farrar, who lack the legs

ABOVE Fans line the Tour of Flanders course leading out of Bruges. LEFT A cycling fan in front of his home on the Tour of Flanders Knokteberg climb, 102 miles into the race.

to go with the bridging attackers. A minute and a half after Belgian Nick Nuyens wins the Tour of Flanders, Farrar storms into Meerbeke and easily takes the field sprint for 13th—three spots outside the UCI points used to rank both riders and teams. Hushovd follows in 53rd place, 4:29 after Nuyens.

After the race, Hushovd tells a Norwegian newspaper reporter that the team suffered because it lacked a clearly defined strategy going into Flanders. Vaughters theorizes Hushovd's judgments may spring from differing cultural expectations. Hushovd joined Garmin-Cervélo when the Cervélo Test Team folded in 2010 and some of its riders merged with Garmin. "He was one of the guys that the Cervélo guys wanted," Vaughters recalls of the circumstances leading to Hushovd's hiring. As Vaughters sees it, his team's "goofy, nerdy nature" does not always suit the Norwegian's more sober-minded personality, and that, in turn, generates frustration.

"I like guys that are intelligent and willing to learn," Vaughters explains. And while Hushovd is both very clever and deeply knowledgeable, "What I'm looking for is smart guys that may be a little bit weird, because a lot of times intelligence goes hand-in-hand with goofiness, especially with bike riders." In his opinion, meshing with such a collection of creatures "was very foreign" for Hushovd.

On the other hand, some riders appreciate the team's respect for sapient nonconformity. As Dan Martin puts it, "I think that's kind of special about

LEFT Dan Lloyd on the Knokteberg. OPPOSITE Heinrich Haussler crosses a field atop the Leberg climb.

this team. The riders have a lot more influence on the tactics in the races. So much is made of the earpieces," he says, in reference to the UCI's radio ban, "but generally I find anyway that in the races I've ridden we make tactical decisions on the road between the riders rather than the directors saying 'do this, do that.'"

As for the public furor over his "no riding" commands, Vaughters is thrilled. The uproar shows that the broadcasts get people engaged at a profound level. Pretending he is a fan watching the Ronde at home who hears "no riding, no riding," Vaughters leans forward and yells at an imaginary TV, "I don't like that!" But, he explains, once fans have time to debate the situation and place it in the larger context of the race—the drama in gambling that other teams will take up the chase reins, and the inanity of burning out your star sprinter by putting him at the front of the field 25 miles from the finish—"it gave a window into the sport at greater depth so they could understand the sport more than they currently do. The way to make cycling an exciting sport is to have people truly understand the tactics," Vaughters continues. Especially in the non-European countries where bike racing is booming as a participant and viewer sport, many fans have "a really superficial understanding of what goes on" in a bike race, which is ultimately not compelling. "That limits the popularity of the sport," he says.

OPPOSITE Tyler Farrar leads the field sprint into Meerbeke to take 13th, the team's top Tour of Flanders placing. RIGHT TOP A team car after being rear-ended by the race medical car at the Tour of Flanders. RIGHT BOTTOM Jonathan Vaughters discusses the team's disappointing Flanders result with team president Matt Johnson.

Water bottles being prepared for the Tour of Flanders.

In America, Vaughters says, "Football is popular because people understand the strategy. They understand calling this play versus this sort of play. And they grow up with that, and they get it." The understanding of football intricacy and strategy that comes through osmosis in American households does not happen when someone falls in love with cycling at 30. "You want to popularize the sport, and you want to have your television ratings go up?" Vaughters concludes with a jab at the UCI. "Getting rid of the radios isn't the way to do it."

THE DAY AFTER FLANDERS, KLIER SITS AT the dining table with Louise Donald. She helps him set up a texting PIN then turns her attention back to a Google Docs spreadsheet. It tracks where all the team's assets—cars, trucks, humans—are at any one time. With races sometimes taking place on three continents at the same time, the color-coded tracking spreadsheet looks like a massive laptop Mondrian. While the always-on Donald is as likely to e-mail at three in the morning as three in the afternoon, Klier draws digital boundaries, shutting off his phone each night at 8:00. "Everybody knows this," he points out matter-of-factly. "They can reach me from seven in the morning until eight in the evening."

Klier, who started racing professionally in 1996, disagrees with Vaughters's radio theories. To make connections with new sponsors, to grow the sport in innovative ways, Klier feels cycling needs shining examples. "You need heroes. America had the luck that they had Lance Armstrong. Germany had for a while the luck that we had Jan Ullrich," the German star who won the Tour de France in 1997 and placed second five times, before retiring in disgrace over a doping scandal. What Klier concludes from the growth of the sport in the United States on Lance Armstrong's success and its rise and fall in Germany on Ullrich's back is that heroes drive the sport's growth.

"A fan looks to the race because he wants to see the fight between Lance Armstrong and Jan Ullrich. They don't care what the sport director is saying in the car." Referring to boxer Muhammad Ali, Klier notes that when he was fighting, "the whole world looked, even if you had no clue about boxing. It didn't matter what the trainer was saying in the corner. They didn't want to see the trainer talking; they wanted to see Muhammad Ali boxing against another star."

THE NIGHT BEFORE SCHELDEPRIJS, A 124-mile race near Antwerp that takes place the Wednesday after Flanders, Johan Vansummeren walks into the Lepelbed. He made it from his home 90 minutes away in the Limburg region of Belgium just in time for dinner. Vansummeren, a loyal domestique whose gentle humility is as prominent as his towering height, quietly remarks, "I've been training like a madman." Donald looks up from her phone and corrects him. "Not *like* a madman, Johan, you *are* a madman."

The next morning, the team bus braves the hurricane-force traffic of Antwerp's ring roads and pulls into a covered parking area near the port city's

fairy-tale, crenelated central square. On the way, the riders peer out at posters showing Tyler Farrar winning last year's Scheldeprijs. Expectations are high that he will do it again, adding his name to the 99-year-old race's list of winners, which includes luminaries Mario Cipollini, Peter van Petegem, and the only three cyclists to have won all five Monuments of cycling (Paris-Roubaix, Liège-Bastogne-Liège, Milan–San Remo, Ronde van Vlaanderen, and the Giro de Lombardia): Belgians Eddy Merckx, Rik van Looy, and Roger de Vlaeminck.

At the mid-morning start, construction workers enjoy cold beers in a street side café. Men and women in bespoke power suits drink beer and orange juice in a VIP area in front of the sign-in stage. It's yet another sunny, warm day, and the usual Belgian race costume of rain jackets, gloves, and tights are not in sight. A smiling Hushovd leans on his bike's handlebars and chats with fellow Norwegian racers Edvald Boasson Hagen and Alexander Kristoff.

Five hours later, the race thunders into a flat sprint finish in the Antwerp bedroom community of Schoten. There's a commotion in the field and Isle

At the Scheldeprijs start in Antwerp, Belgium, Thor Hushovd shares a laugh with compatriots Edvald Boasson Hagen and Alexander Kristoff.

of Man super sprinter Mark Cavendish emerges at full speed from the scrum for the win.

Farrar is nowhere to be found. Team soigneur Sandra Ni Hodnae rushes up, a mammoth backpack and red bag of drinks weighing her down. Distressed, she asks, "Have you seen Tyler? He went down."

Within sight of the finish line, Farrar's close friend and Belgian training partner Wouter Weylandt lost control in the frenzied sprint, and Farrar crashed with him. While the two only suffer bruises and road rash, another crasher, Belgian Sjef De Wilde, is loaded into an ambulance with a broken neck and head injuries. Later that night, Farrar walks stiffly into the Lepelbed dining room, his arm and leg covered with fresh Tegaderm bandages. "I could be better," he says, wincing. The day is a reminder of the trauma and catastrophe, the life-and-death consequences, crouching in wait beneath the riders' idyllic workaday existence.

RIGHT Peter van Petegem, Marya Pongrace, Tyler Farrar, and Louise Donald (left to right) review footage of Farrar's crash from the final meters of Scheldeprijs. BELOW Johan Vansummeren before a Paris-Roubaix reconnaissance ride.

That evening, Farrar watches a replay of the finish with Marya Pongrace and Van Petegem. Farrar can't know it at the moment, but the video playing across Pongrace's Macintosh screen prefigures an event that, in 33 short days, will end 26-year-old Weylandt's life at the Giro d'Italia.

THE DAY AFTER SCHELDEPRIJS, THE TEAM moves to France. It's Paris-Roubaix time. The squad installs itself at the Dolce Chantilly hotel, a sprawling, Gatsbyesque fantasy of a place set in a forest 25 miles north of Paris. The Hell of the North is the most iconic one-day race on the calendar, and as such, it attracts the sort of team sponsors and

VIPs who appreciate plush lodgings and bucolic settings. Hotel bar conversations revolve around the best first-class airline service to Europe, the finest hotels in Paris and Aspen, private schools in Manhattan, and a quantitative investment analysis conference in Switzerland. Not top of mind for pro cyclists, but quotidian for some of those who underwrite their sport.

Dating back to 1896, Paris-Roubaix is a flat, 160-mile race that drags the peloton like a chunk of parmesan over 32 grating miles of wretched cobblestone farm roads. Its nickname refers to the hellish appearance of the landscape after the trench warfare of World War I. Its primitive roads, often horrific weather, and the fact that it has been won by some of the most revered names in cycling give it an appeal at once sublimely regal and grossly primitive.

While the mechanics have been preparing for this race since January, the Thursday before the Sunday race, head mechanic Geoff Brown and his team set up shop in the Dolce hotel parking lot and make final preparations. For the mechanics, the year is "one big stage race," Brown says, describing their life driving and flying from one race to another for 10 months of the year. And because they use the same type of bikes and wheels, "one race flows into the other." From the mechanic's point of view, "it's only the riders that ever change." But, says Brown, "when you go to Paris-Roubaix, you have to actually deviate."

Roubaix's cobblestone roads were designed for plodding horse-drawn wagons made of heavy timber and iron ore, not gossamer plastic bicycles on spider-webbed wheels. Because the course so taxes equipment, Roubaix demands reinforced frames, tough wheels, and extra-wide tubular

ABOVE Doug Ellis (left) and Jonathan Vaughters at the Dolce Chantilly, the team's hotel for Paris-Roubaix. LEFT In the Dolce lobby, Matt Johnson, Jon Cassat, Alex Palmer, Eric Bernard, and Caroline Murphy-Lassuie (left to right) discuss Garmin's Tour de France marketing plans.

tires handmade in France at $300 a pop. "It's a special date," Brown reverently observes. "A very special date."

It's so exceptional that Garmin's Jon Cassat flies in from Kansas City. He is meeting Garmin France managers Eric Bernard and Caroline Murphy-Lassuie along with Matt Johnson and Alex Palmer. The five sit in the richly appointed hotel lobby, where a waitress delivers cappuccinos, milk in a delicate porcelain pitcher, and rock candy sticks that look like bejeweled shepherd's staffs. Cassat asks, "What do we do for the Tour this year to make it a big deal?" Johnson points out that having world champion Hushovd on the team "makes a huge difference." The Norwegian's rainbow jersey makes him a subject of intense media interest with both the international cycling and mainstream press. Any news coverage that focuses on how Hushovd uses Garmin products provides a twofold return; it gets the Garmin name in the public eye, and it provides an implicit endorsement for their products.

The meeting carries on for two hours, ranging from mapping out how Garmin can generate fan interest online by uploading rider power output data to how it can get T-shirts in the hands of journalists in provincial France. "What about video?" Murphy-Lassuie asks. Palmer sinks back in his seat—this is a sticky issue. The public is thirsty for video vignettes into their heroes' lives. However, these opportunities come at a cost. Slipstream and Garmin staff have to constantly be on hand to feed the online machine, and in the case of race video, Tour owner ASO precludes anyone, teams included, from using any race video—no matter who takes it—without first paying ASO to license the content.

The next day, the team heads out to pre-ride part of the course. A Norwegian TV crew greets the bus's arrival in a supermarket parking lot. Farrar steps out with a paper cup of espresso, while Vansummeren studies his mobile phone on the other side of a team car. Norwegian Gabriel Rasch (a loyal 35-year-old Hushovd lieutenant who looks all of 25) adjusts his handlebar alignment with mechanic Kris Withington. Sep Vanmarcke is smiling as always, while Hushovd is alone with his thoughts at the parking lot entrance. Behind him, Schoonaker orders a stack of pizzas for the staff from a roadside pizza kiosk. The TV crew interviews Van Petegem about what it's like to be directing a team eight years after winning the event himself.

Along with the rest of the Roubaix team—Hammond, Haussler, Brett Lancaster, and Klier—the team rolls out of the parking lot with Vaughters and Van Petegem in a car behind. It's sunny. Dust blows over the cobbles. At the end of one stretch of *pavé*, the riders skirt a spreading pool of black motor oil, a glistening reminder of how these jagged, heavily crowned paths rip the bottoms out of passenger cars.

The next morning, light spills from the mechanics' trucks in the predawn dark. Dew glistens on the Cervélos, lovingly prepared and loaded on the team cars. Coolers in the back of the Skodas are filled with bottles, eight-ounce cans of Coke, and tiny foil-wrapped sandwiches. Mechanics Brown, Alex Banyay, Withington, and Pozak mill about, drinking steaming espressos from the truck's coffee machine. Except for the voices of Van Petegem and fellow team director Lionel Marie, who have a knack for finding laughter and sunshine in any

Energy bars for Paris-Roubaix in the team bus.

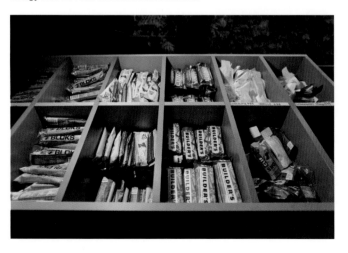

occasion, all is calm. No last-minute scurrying about pumping tires and filling bottles.

While the pink fingers of dawn begin to trace the eastern sky, soigneur Ni Hodnae walks across the hotel parking lot with an armload of baguettes. They are the foundation of sandwiches to feed the staff and VIPs who will follow the race. Pulled from a Chantilly baker's oven within the last hour, the still-warm loaves radiate the heavenly aroma of France.

In the hotel dining room, Farrar sits for breakfast, his arm wrapped in fresh white bandages and his leg crusted with scabs from Wednesday's tumble. The rest of the riders filter in and eat eggs, fruit, and oatmeal in silence. The tension is palpable. The team that, to its discomfort, was labeled as the classics killer, still hasn't produced. Even Internet sniping about the team's failure to

deliver at Flanders has them down. The night Farrar crashes at Scheldeprijs, Klier vents, pointing out that, relative to other teams, Garmin-Cervélo does not have a string of classics *winners*. "Go down the list," he says of his team's record at the classics. Compared with teams like Quick-Step and Leopard, Garmin-Cervélo has "top 10s, but no wins."

Hammond, Hushovd, Haussler, and Vansummeren have all placed in the top 10 at Roubaix in the past. The team knows this race, and with the eyes of both the world and the sponsors at an adjoining table on them, they know they only have so many chances left to deliver on that promise. Outside the dining room window, the orange disk of the sun oozes over the horizon and sets the morning golf course fog aglow. A schedule on the riders' table reads, "Breakfast, 6:30. Leave by bus 7:55. Neutral

ABOVE LEFT At dawn on the day of Paris-Roubaix, soigneur Sandra Ni Hodnae carries warm baguettes for sandwiches for the staff and VIPs. ABOVE Directeurs sportifs Peter van Petegem and Lionel Marie cut the tension at sunrise on the morning of Paris-Roubaix.

kilometers: 3." And at the bottom, someone, not a native English speaker, has scrawled: "Be relax but FOCUS. You are a TEAM READY. Cheers, The Staff."

At the race start in Compiègne it isn't hard to find Americans who fit the Garmin advertising demographic. Beneath the golden-hued walls of the ornate and imposing Château de Compiègne, a royal residence first built for France's King Charles V in the fourteenth century, Ken Meadows presses against a fence and watches the riders sign in.

Meadows flew to Europe from Long Island, New York, so his wife could run the Paris Marathon while he watches Paris-Roubaix. Both the Paris Marathon and Paris-Roubaix are organized by Tour de France owner ASO. "I've always been involved in sports where you have to torture yourself to be successful," Meadows says. He's wearing an Ironman triathlon hat and has been following cycling for 10 years. "I love to watch these guys turn themselves inside out." Pointing at the whippet-thin pros bumping

Bus driver Andrea Bisogno awaits Johan Vansummeren's arrival in the Roubaix velodrome.

across the cobbled plaza, Meadows says, "The pain that they go through has to be internalized for them to be successful, as opposed to just pure agility and talent like most American sports."

Five feet from the team bus, Dave Hollander and his son Noah dangle a Colorado state flag over a barrier. Hollander is from the affluent ski town of Aspen. The Hollanders also represent the educated, worldly demographic sweet spot advertisers yearn to reach. Hollander has been a close aficionado of the team "from the beginning," he says. Soaking in the morning sun, he adds, "I really like what Vaughters is doing. In the beginning he built the team very slowly instead of trying to buy a team. And, obviously, his philosophy that we are going to try to have a clean team." Putting his hand on Noah's shoulder, Hollander says, "That's the philosophy that I want him to have."

AFTER THE ARENBERG FOREST SECTION OF cobblestones, 108 miles into the 160-mile race, Vansummeren bridges up to an earlier breakaway. In the field, 2010 Roubaix winner Fabian Cancellara attacks with 23 miles remaining. Hushovd marks him, sitting on the Swiss rider's wheel and not pulling through. It is a textbook team strategy. Hushovd forces the race favorite, who has no teammates around him, to burn more energy chasing from the front of the field. If Cancellara does catch the break, Hushovd gets a free ride in his draft, leaving the Norwegian with fresher legs for the sprint.

But then, 19 miles from the finish, Cancellara sits up. Frustrated, he waves his hand at Vaughters's

Johan Vansummeren on the Paris-Roubaix cobbles.

Garmin-Cervélo car like a man washing windows, then points at the world champion. In 2010, Cancellara was indomitable and rode away from everyone. This year, Hushovd's tenacity neuters those tactics. If no one is going to help, Cancellara is not riding. The break's gap quickly swells from

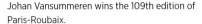
Johan Vansummeren wins the 109th edition of Paris-Roubaix.

25 seconds to 40. Then, with 10 miles remaining, Vansummeren attacks his breakaway companions on the 1.3-mile Carrefour de l'Arbre cobbles. In short order the Limburger is away, alone with nothing but his thoughts, the roaring crowd, and 9 miles of road between the present and a Paris-Roubaix victory.

The team staff paces nervously on the velodrome infield. Bus driver Andrea Bisogno sits on an ice chest and watches a big screen above the west end of the velodrome. "It's so far," he frets. Vansummeren's rangy frame labors away. Covered in filth, teeth blackened, shoulders bobbing—on the contrasty video screen, the Belgian looks like a nineteenth-century laborer riding home from a shift in one of the grim textile mills that made Roubaix a cradle of the French Industrial Revolution.

Vansummeren's girlfriend, Jasmine Vangrieken, watches, too, clutches her head, and paces. Will "Summie," as her 30-year-old boyfriend is called, make the right-hand turn into the velodrome before he is caught by Cancellara, who has now dropped Hushovd? Will his madman training regime be enough to keep him off the front?

The exulting crowd does not know it, but as Vansummeren turns off the tree-lined Avenue Alfred Motte onto the velodrome access road, he corners gingerly; with Cancellara bearing down on him like a Swiss bullet, Vansummeren's rear tire has been going flat for the last 3 miles. And then, Vansummeren is on the track, paddling like a towering, wheeled stick figure through hot white light reflecting off the velodrome banks. The crowd's cheering doubles,

a big wave overtaking a smaller one, then dumps in a thundering roar as the Belgian carves his first turn around the velodrome. Electrifying.

Vansummeren passes the thick blue finish line, and a track steward hammers the one-lap-to-go bell. The man from Lommel dares a glance over his shoulder. Then it's done. He crosses the line, his jersey a carapace of dried mud and salt. Fists thrust in the air, Vansummeren rides around the apron, when suddenly Vangrieken is running next to him, gliding like an angel with flowing red hair, followed by a black mob of photographers. She takes her man's filthy face between her manicured hands, kisses him through furrows of wretched cobble muck. Andreas Klier approaches. A gigantic smile cracks the crust of grime on his face; his wish for cycling heroes comes true today.

The team is a classics winner manqué no more. As he stands on the velodrome infield, Vaughters's thumbs fly over the keyboard of his BlackBerry. His first Tweet? "He who laughs last, laughs hardest," he says, turning to a bristling array of microphones. Garmin's Cassat is beside himself; "How was *that*?" he exclaims. Doug Ellis, the cycling enthusiast whose largesse over the last half decade culminates in this moment, sits quietly on a barstool improbably deposited in the infield. He pecks at his phone. Though the stadium is cacophonous with the jackhammering voice of French announcer Daniel Mangeas, Ellis quietly absorbs his team's apotheosis.

OPPOSITE Moments after his Paris-Roubaix win Vansummeren's girlfriend, Jasmine Vangrieken, wipes grime from his lips; shortly thereafter she will become his fiancée.

Soigneur Ni Hodnae whisks Vansummeren to an area behind the podium that is closed to all media, save a couple of TV cameras. She wraps a towel around his waist and, like a surfer donning a wetsuit in a beach parking lot, Vansummeren drops his bib shorts and changes into a fresh pair for the podium. Vaughters appears. Both men clench and shake their fists at their sides, a mutual expression of the consummation of a life's work, and then the victor sweeps up his director in a twisting embrace. Ni Hodnae towels off Vansummeren's beaming face, swipes grime from his neck, and hands him a fresh top and baseball cap. Seconds before a handler guides Vansummeren to the podium, Matt Johnson hands him a pair of white Transitions sunglasses for the images about to be beamed into cycling eternity.

While Vansummeren collects his Roubaix cobblestone trophy, pees in a bottle for the drug testers, and fulfills his press conference obligations—and asks Jasmine to marry him along the way—the team celebrates in the bus. Hushovd, Farrar, Vanmarcke, and Rasch slump on couches, while Haussler stands, looking on with an impish grin. Beers all around. Hushovd studies the label on his bottle and exchanges it for another brand. The riders are at once euphoric and exhausted by their six-hour day in the saddle.

At last Vansummeren parts the black curtains at the bottom of the bus's stairs. Like an ostrich peering over a fence, his head pops up into the aisle, and the team cheers. Team doctor Serge Niamke hands him a Belgian beer. He takes a deep pull, shakes his head at the taste of it all, and beams. Merry prankster Haussler hands Vansummeren a pen and jersey and asks him to sign it with a bon mot that would

make a coal miner blush. Hushovd stands and hugs Vansummeren, repeating, "Incredible, incredible." The Norwegian placed third here in 2009 and second in 2010. The team win is sweet, but not moving up a notch on the podium himself is bitter. Later, Vaughters tells me, "Thor was the reason that we won Paris-Roubaix." Hushovd played the role of the perfect domestique, and, says Vaughters, "He was the only guy that could follow Cancellara." But, he adds, Hushovd "was never going to win, no matter what tactic we played. If you look at the final, Cancellara still drops him in the end."

A FEW DAYS AFTER THE RACE, TEAM OWNER Ellis reflects on the moment from his home in New York City. What was he thinking as Vansummeren plowed those final miles into Roubaix? "Matt was there, and Gerard was there, and Jon Cassat was there," Ellis recalls of the Slipstream president, the Cervélo cofounder Gerard Vroomen, and the Garmin executive. "It was super emotional for all of us." He adds, "There is always some degree of disbelief and fear the thing that you want to have happen isn't going to happen." Watching the final kilometers on a velodrome TV was troubling for Ellis. "It was really difficult for me to have something that I really want, and am in a position of maybe getting, and yet still there's time for it to all fall apart."

Some of that emotion stems from Ellis's relationship with Vansummeren. After Paris-Roubaix

Andreas Klier at the Paris-Roubaix finish.

LEFT Jonathan Vaughters greets Johan Vansummeren after his Roubaix win. ABOVE Team owner Doug Ellis hoists the Roubaix trophy.

in 2010, where the tall Belgian did not finish (after a promising eighth place in 2008 and fifth in 2009 while riding for Davitamon-Lotto), Vansummeren approached Ellis. "He came up to me after the race and he said, 'Sorry Doug, I really let you down. I know this is why you hired me.'" To which Ellis recalls responding, "Look Johan, we hired you because we knew you'd be strong in a race like this, but we understand these things happen. We didn't hire you just for this race; we hired you because you are a great teammate."

Johnson wastes no time getting photos of Vansummeren holding the *pavé* trophy aloft into his sponsor pitches. Vaughters also incorporates the image into his team representations; the week after Roubaix, on April 23, he gives a presentation at an innovation conference, TEDx, in Bermuda, where he talks about his efforts to reform cycling. He couches the story of his project to clean up and change the cycling business in the history of the team, from his eureka moment as a pro that cycling was corrupt with doping to his decision to start a new American-based squad that would ride clean all the way to the Tour de France. And the presentation, of course, closes with images of Vansummeren winning the Queen of the Classics.

Vaughters says Vansummeren does not have the typical winner's qualities. He can't climb, and he can't sprint. But he has enormous strength and endurance. "He is just as fast after seven hours as he is after two hours." In addition, his unique physique suits the singular idiosyncrasies of Paris-Roubaix. Vaughters thinks he can win it again. In fact, it is the *only* race he thinks Vansummeren is likely to win.

Vaughters explains that Paris-Roubaix is totally flat and really rough in the places where attacks go. Because of the cobbles, Vaughters says, "the critical moments are performed at 40K an hour, not 60." At 40 kph (25 mph), Vansummeren's lanky frame does not hinder him to the same degree it does at 60 kph. This is pure aerodynamics; the power required to push his tall frontal area through the air on a flat road quadruples with a doubling of speed. Put another way, when Vansummeren attacked over the cobbles of the Carrefour de l'Arbe, he could stay away at 22 mph, whereas in a typical road race on smooth roads, a pro would have to go away at nearly twice that speed, requiring four times more power. "All of a sudden, his lack of aerodynamics is irrelevant," says Vaughters, while Vansummeren's ability to keep his engine pinned at its enormous power peak is totally relevant. When you slow everyone down, as the cobbles do in this race, "the fact that he's stronger than everyone else comes to the fore," Vaughters says. "It's really unique in that it's a pan-flat race

TOP Johan Vansummeren celebrates his Paris-Roubaix win in the team bus. BOTTOM Heinrich Haussler has Vansummeren sign his jersey while team doctor Serge Niamke looks on.

where the decisive moments are at 35 to 40 km an hour," he adds. "And that's the reason that Johan Vansummeren is so good at that race."

As for Vansummeren, what was he thinking as he rode down Avenue Alfred Motte toward the velodrome finish? Another type of air pressure entirely. "I felt nothing," he recalls with a shake of his head. "I did not even hear the crowd. I was too worried about my tire. 'Fuck, fuck, fuck, fuck, fuck,' I was thinking." He stares at me. A leaking tire with 3 miles to go while off the front at Roubaix. "Stress. That was stress."

Paris-Roubaix winner Johan Vansummeren with second place Fabian Cancellera and third place Maaren Tjallingii.

THE ARDENNES CLASSICS 3

The cobbles are done. Now the classics move to the hillier races: Amstel Gold in Holland and La Flèche Wallonne and Liège-Bastogne-Liège in Belgium's southern Wallonia region. Away from the tourist destinations of Brussels and Bruges, the team's hotel in 1,000-year-old Genk is nestled among the rural landscapes of Limburg, a region in eastern Belgium dressed in the soft white flowers of cherry and pear trees. It is April 16, the Saturday before the Amstel Gold Race, which starts 13 miles and a country away in Maastricht, Holland. As a Japanese bike tourist with a floppy hat and alarmingly worn-out tires looks on from the hotel entry, the Amstel squad gathers for a 90-minute spin. Limburg local Vansummeren is piloting.

Stroking his chin, directeur sportif Johnny Weltz suggests a route. "You go up the hill past the church then turn at the roundabout." Vansummeren waves off the proposal like a gnat, "No, we won't see any hot chicks if we go that way." Weltz laughs. "Oooof . . . that's good, you should only enjoy the birds and the trees!"

With the team heading into the second half of the Spring Classics, the vibe is palpably less stressful than it was two weeks ago. There are no VIPs at this peaceful lakeside hotel. Other than the bike tourist, no fans crowd the mechanics' truck and pester the riders for autographs. With his can of Red Bull next to an iPod dock, mechanic Alex Banyay can assemble Ryder Hesjedal's bike in relative tranquility. After Roubaix, "All we need is a Tour de France stage win, and we can pack it in for the season," Banyay observes. He's joking—sort of. The fact is that a win at Roubaix and the Tour would make a season more successful than most teams could ever hope for.

David Millar arrives at 2:30 that afternoon. Sporting a porkpie hat, skateboarder shoes, and a sport coat, he looks like a Santa Monica hipster. Someone says, "David, you look like a tourist." Millar, who at 34 is the only British rider to have worn the leader's jersey in all three grand tours, is not amused. Lufthansa lost his bike on the 90-minute flight from Milan to Brussels. Cell phone pressed to his ear, he politely presses the agent to locate it before tomorrow morning's race. A few feet away, directeurs sportifs Eric van Lancker and Lionel Marie sit on lobby couches with Joachim

The mechanics clean the bikes after every training ride.

TOP Johan Vansummeren, Michel Kreder, Eric van Lancker, and Johnny Weltz (left to right) in Genk, Belgium. BOTTOM Mechanic Joan Linares and Ryder Hesjedal unpack Hesjedal's bike for the Amstel Gold Race.

Schoonaker. Flipping through a calendar of historical racing images by longtime cycling photographer John Pierce, they identify photos without a glance at the captions. "Malcolm Elliott, must be the Tour—'87!"

Team chiropractor Kevin Reichlin returns from a run. "I ran to Holland," he says. He looks from the trio to the calendar. "What are we waiting for?"

"For the day to end," Schoonaker responds. "That is what we are always waiting for."

Hair wet from his post-ride shower, Vansummeren steps out of the elevator with a mesh bag of dirty laundry. He hands it to soigneur Alyssa

Morahan. He will get the cleaned clothes back tomorrow at breakfast. The Roubaix winner spies the local newspaper *Het Belang Van Limburg* on the reception desk. Along with Ronde van Vlaanderen winner Nick Nuyens, his own face stares back at him from a centerfold photo spread. In an accompanying interview, the writer asks Vansummeren how Vaughters's system is different from others. "Look how he's dressed," Vansummeren says. He tells the writer that some of the e-mails from his American boss are also different, asking the Belgian things like "Help me, my girlfriend is ten years younger, what do I do?" The weekend paper includes a glossy

24-page magazine insert about Vansummeren and his fiancée, including a fashion photo feature, an article on his upbringing, and a photo of him, Vangrieken, and his Porsche. The six days between now and last Sunday in Roubaix were "Crazy, man. So busy!"

While Vansummeren reads, Morahan, an American who lives in the northern Spanish province of Cantabria, heads up to a hotel room set aside for massage. Ryder Hesjedal lies on his stomach on the massage table. Though Morahan works his leg and back muscles like she's softening a slab of abalone, the Canadian dozes off during his daily recovery massage. Morahan was once interviewed for an article that called her a masseuse. She was not happy. "Masseuse," she protests, "makes me think of a tiny lady standing on someone's back. I'm a massage therapist!"

The next morning Reichlin and team doctor Adrie van Diemen depart Maastricht's atmospheric Market Square 15 minutes before the riders. A policeman clears a path for their car through the square, which is crammed with Amstel Gold spectators on this sunny Sunday morning. Vansummeren rides next to the car and grabs the roof. A woman pressed up against the barriers recognizes him and swoons with delight.

Today, Reichlin and Van Diemen are supporting the team with spare wheels and water bottles at several points along the 162-mile route of this 46th edition of the race. Van Diemen is a Dutch physiologist who has worked in cycling for nearly three decades. He also trains speed skaters. With a shock of curly hair and an elastic face that indexes his easygoing demeanor, the 50-year-old Dutchman

is fascinated by the economics of pro cycling. He rattles off figures. It costs $34 to reach a consumer through Formula One motor racing and $1.43 to reach a consumer through pro cycling. Compared with other pro sports, cycling is "an absolutely ridiculously cheap sport to invest in," he says.

Van Diemen notes that the culture of pro cycling is changing. Thirty years ago doctors focused on improving rider performance through training. Lowering his eyes, he adds that with the advent of doping, "It all got medical and training was just secondary." Now he sees the sport and its health practitioners moving away from its success-through-pharmaceuticals past. Doctors are going back to their calling, "keeping the guys healthy."

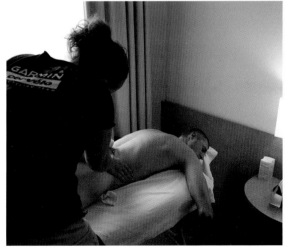

TOP At the team's hotel in Genk, Johan Vansummeren reads about his Paris-Roubaix victory. BOTTOM Soigneur Alyssa Morahan massages Ryder Hesjedal in Genk.

Chiropractor Kevin Reichlin (left) and physician Adrie van Diemen wait to hand off water bottles atop the Vijlenerbos, the 14th of 32 climbs in the Amstel Gold Race.

take his position with wheels and bottles at a nearby climb, Reichlin explains that supplements can be problematic. "It's not a regulated industry like the pharmaceutical industry," Reichlin explains. "If a vitamin and mineral company says, 'My bottle of vitamins contains these ingredients,' nobody tests it to say that's exactly what's in there."

So the team takes that task upon itself. Reichlin cites amino acid supplements. A significant body of medical literature suggests that for athletes who do intense training, amino acids help the body adapt to training stress. When he needs to replenish the team's amino acid supplements, Reichlin says, "I call the company that makes it, and I say, 'I want to order 120 bottles. And I want them all to be from the same lot.'"

Once the team receives the shipment, a medical staff member ensures every bottle is stamped with the same lot number then sends one bottle to HFL Sports Science, a team sponsor and independent testing lab in Britain. HFL tests the product for purity. "As long as that is clean," Reichlin explains, "then I know the entire lot is clean."

All this is a significant investment in time, effort, and money, but Reichlin says there is no other way to ensure riders are not inadvertently ingesting something that could harm them. Indeed, as Vaughters tells the riders repeatedly throughout the year, if they make a bad decision, they will not only affect their livelihoods, but they will eliminate every rider's and staff member's job.

Image and practical concerns also fostered the team's no-needle policy. Van Diemen explains that it used to be standard practice for athletes to get intravenous fluids after taxing days on the bike.

Reichlin has been with the team since 2003 and says he is motivated to stay because he adores cycling and because Slipstream allows him to pursue a passion. "I've always loved the challenge of healing people without medication," he says. The Boulder, Colorado–based chiropractor adds, "Particularly with a team that's clean, I really get to see that happening."

As part of his job, Reichlin helps govern the team's use of nutritional supplements. Sipping a cappuccino in the warm Dutch sun while waiting to

The Garmin-Cervélo team does not do this for two reasons. One, a needle in an athlete's vein is not a wholesome image. And two, research shows that the best way to rehydrate is orally. If a rider is so dehydrated he needs an IV, Reichlin says, "He should be in the hospital."

The first wheel and water handoff spot is Amstel Gold's 14th climb of the day, the Vijlenerbos. It's a perfect spring day; the air is soft to the point of tactility. Across the road, a couple looking to be in their 80s sit on camp stools in their Sunday best, he in a suit and tie, she in a dress. The peloton appears across a valley then passes in a steadily climbing group. Vande Velde, Hesjedal, Michel Kreder, Murilo Fischer—all look relaxed. Only 85 miles into the 162-mile race, they are a ways from the point where they will begin racing in a bid to deliver Hesjedal to the finish one spot ahead of last year's second. After another uneventful support stop in Huls, 60 miles from the finish, Reichlin and Van Diemen head for the finish in the town of Valkenberg, where the field climbs the Cauberg three times.

The Cauberg is one of the world's great cycling parties. Picture a forested trench that climbs upward for just shy of 2 miles. Line the bottom with bars, cafés, and house parties. Throw in thousands of cycling-mad fans from all over Belgium and Holland, and, for good measure, put a casino at the top of the climb. Add to that a giant TV showing a live feed of the race action and drench the air with techno music from the aforementioned bars. Then have a Dutch beer conglomerate sponsor the

Holland's Amstel Gold Race.

shindig and dress the climb with beer tents and the podium girls in frocks made of beer coasters. That is the spirit of Amstel Gold.

The day is not Garmin-Cervélo's. Hesjedal rolls in 141st, over 14 minutes behind winner Philippe Gilbert and well behind the highest-placing Garmin-Cervélo rider, Brazilian national champion Fischer in 28th.

At the team bus, Vansummeren is already showered and signing autographs; he abandoned the race early. Vande Velde's father, two-time U.S. Olympic cyclist John Vande Velde, pushes a stroller with his two granddaughters. Christian threads his way through the gathered fans and his daughters call out, "Daddy!"

Hesjedal's race ends with about 40 miles remaining when intestinal problems strike. He checks with the race doctor who travels with the race in progress, but once the bowels let loose, there isn't much a doc in a convertible can do, and Hesjedal is out of contention. His case of the touristas is so bad that at one point he gets off his bike and knocks on the front door of a house. "I had to ask this Dutch lady if I could use the bathroom," he recounts after the race. Shrugging his shoulders, he says, "When you've got to go, you've got to go."

Reichlin says bowel problems like Hesjedal's are not uncommon with finely tuned elite cyclists, though they are more frequent in marathoners, because they suffer more jarring. Holding his hands vertically and parallel to one another, Reichlin rotates them in a circular motion like a cyclist's feet. "You or me, if you tilt us a little bit"—he angles his hands a few degrees to the right—"we can handle it. Not these guys."

THE DAY AFTER AMSTEL, SOME OF THE riders visit new team sponsor DSM, a Dutch materials and life-sciences company in Urmond, Holland. On the bus ride Millar sleeps in the back. Hesjedal sits in the front and watches the Low Countries stream past. Barges float down canals. Girls in white dresses ride sturdy black bikes down flower-lined bike paths. Windmills turn. The Zen-like Canadian does not show distress about his crummy day at Amstel. Going in, he wanted to better last year's second place, but nature conspired against him. "Ahhhh, you know . . ." he says at an adagio pace. "It's just one of those things."

Vansummeren and his fiancée, Vangrieken, are waiting in the DSM parking lot. After letting Millar take his Porsche for a quick spin, Vansummeren pulls his Paris-Roubaix trophy—a cobblestone mounted on a base—from the trunk and heads toward a group of about 20 employees waiting outside the front door with cameras poised. Weltz pulls up in a team car with Martijn Maaskant, one of two Dutch riders on the team, along with Kreder. Iris Slappendel from the women's team has also come over from her home in Holland.

A raised platform is set up beneath real palm trees in a white atrium in DSM's office building. Vansummeren asks his fiancée to join him on the stage. Queried about Roubaix and his simultaneous marriage proposal, Vansummeren holds Vangrieken's hand and explains that while most propose with a diamond, he did it with a cobblestone Roubaix trophy. "Rocks are forever," he says, grinning. The crowd is delighted.

The moderator asks David Millar if he's looking forward to the London Olympics in 2012. With a tinge of bitterness, Millar responds that he would be if he were not banned from the event. He spares the attendees the details: In 2004 Millar confessed to using EPO in 2001 and 2003. He sat out of the sport for two years as punishment, renounced his former ways, and signed on with Vaughters's team in 2008. But the British Olympic Association bans doping offenders for life from the Olympics.

The master of ceremonies recovers with an awkward laugh and then unknowingly heads into another pro cycling political thicket. He asks about a new Tour of Beijing in October. He recounts bringing a Chinese colleague to the Amstel Gold Race. "If all the billions of Chinese are just as excited, there will be a lot of audience there."

While Millar is too polite to highlight it on stage, the moderator unwittingly touches on a building storm in pro cycling. To protest the UCI's ban on race radios, the AIGCP—the organization of teams that Vaughters runs—has threatened to boycott the Chinese race in October. That race is organized by Global Cycling Promotion, a UCI-owned organization. While the race recognizes China's enormous market potential, it is a UCI-orchestrated event that the teams can use as a platform to make their voices heard. Choosing another established race to boycott, as the riders threatened to do at February's Omloop Het Nieuwsblad, would hurt the race organizer more than the UCI. And in the case of the Belgian one-day Omloop Het Nieuwsblad, it would affect Flanders Classics, a race organizer that, as the Flanders TV coverage shows, is willing to experiment with race radios. (In the end the UCI

Brazilian national champion Murilo Fischer, the team's top finisher at Amstel.

LEFT Mechanic Joan Linares awaits the start of La Flèche Wallonne in Charleroi, Belgium. BELOW David Millar before Flèche Wallonne.

the 1970s. Navigating past the blackened steel works and coal mines surrounding Charleroi, the bus parks in the shadow of nineteenth-century brick row houses. Vande Velde steps out into the brilliant spring sunshine and is mobbed by autograph seekers. Millar takes a phone call from behind the curtained bus steps. Climbers Dan Martin, Peter Stetina, and Christophe Le Mével join Millar, Vande Velde, Hesjedal, Kreder, and Fischer at the sign-in board in front of the Charleroi soccer stadium. As riders mass for the start of the hilly, 125-mile one-day semiclassic, Belgian climbing specialist Maxime Monfort of the Leopard Trek team asks Hesjedal how he feels after his intestinal problems at Amstel. The Canadian says he's good and recounts his stop at a Dutch house to use the toilet. "Really?" Monfort replies, impressed. There is fraternity here.

Le Mével messes with his bike's brakes at the start. Something is amiss. The Frenchman cocks his head and speaks into the radio microphone under his jersey. Mechanic Joan Linares appears out of nowhere with a three-pronged Allen wrench. He fiddles with the brakes then tells Le Mével to follow him. The race is set to start in seconds, but Le Mével rides away. A minute later he reappears with functioning brakes. He sprints after the departing field.

Like Amstel Gold, La Flèche Wallonne finishes on a climb—the cruelly steep Mur de Huy. At the race start Stetina says, "I like this finish better than Liège." Its taxing incline suits the Colorado rider. The hill is also a massive party. Beer tents keep fans lubricated, while they wave giant flags over the word *Huy*, which is stenciled in italics all the way up the climb. Brick houses on the 20 percent incline are like Lego structures, footings defying

the dizzying descent. Fans hang out of windows or barbecue sausages in yards. More than a race, this is cycling ritual, a feast, a Wednesday breaking of the bonds of daily life.

The racing action is nonstop, because both the pro women and men race today. The women go up the Mur twice and the men three times. Fans don't have to wait long before seeing another shattered field struggle through.

The day is something of a disappointment for the team. On the final ascent, Le Mével enters the bottom of the nearly mile-long climb in third position, but fades to ninth by the finish. His result is the team's

best, and in the last 500 meters the Frenchman's face is a roar of effort as he finishes alongside 2010 Flèche victor Cadel Evans, Olympic gold medalist Sammy Sanchez, and Tour de France winner Alberto Contador. The only French rider on the team, Le Mével always seems content. "He's a French guy who wants to be on a foreign team," Vaughters explains. "He's adventuresome and wants to see a bit more of the world." Additionally, Vaughters, who rode with French squad Crédit Agricole as a pro, says French teams "tend to be 28 individuals." With Garmin-Cervélo, Le Mével "likes the team atmosphere, he likes that we really come together."

LEFT Minutes before the Flèche Wallonne start, Christophe Le Mével discusses a brake problem with Joan Linares. ABOVE David Millar signs autographs in Charleroi.

Flèche Wallonne sign-in at Charleroi stadium: Dan Martin, Christophe Le Mével, David Millar, Peter Stetina, Ryder Hesjedal, Michel Kreder (left to right).

Dan Martin crashes 44 miles into the race, when his cousin Nicolas Roche eats it in front of him while descending from the first ascent of the Mur de Huy. After the race, Van Diemen sends Martin to the hospital for X-rays. "It's a shame," the Dutch doctor says. "He was training so hard for this race." The Mur is the type of finish that suits Martin best.

As a team car inches past on its way to the hospital, Martin cradles his elbow in the passenger seat and winks. The X-rays find no broken bones. "For now," Van Diemen cautions.

On the bus, Le Mével emerges from the shower with a towel around his waist. As the Frenchman vigorously dries his hair, Vande Velde congratulates

TOP LEFT Peter Stetina passes a police officer on the Mur de Huy. TOP RIGHT Dan Martin seconds before crashing on his first descent of the Mur de Huy. LEFT Ryder Hesjedal placed 13th at Flèche Wallonne.

TOP Clif Bars tucked away for the race. ABOVE Michel Kreder (left) and Ryder Hesjedal on the bus in Huy after Flèche Wallonne. TOP RIGHT Maxime Monfort with Ryder Hesjedal at Flèche Wallonne.

him on the top 10 finish: "You were strong, man." Hesjedal, who places 13th, is his usual ethereal self. With feet propped up on a long bench seat, Michel Kreder eyes the Canadian as he walks past in sandals, sweatpants, and a base layer shirt with the sleeves torn off. In the back of the bus, Peter Stetina isn't happy. He finished 6:22 off of Philippe Gilbert's winning time. Asked how the day went, the 24-year-old just shakes his head.

But it's only Wednesday. Sunday offers another chance.

THE FRIDAY BEFORE SUNDAY'S LIÈGE-Bastogne-Liège, Vande Velde, Hesjedal, Le Mével, Martin, and Stetina pre-ride the final 100 kilometers of the hilly course in the Belgian Ardennes. Director Eric van Lancker follows in a team car with mechanic Alex Banyay. As the riders head up the first climb of the day, the nearly 2-mile-long Côte de Wanne, Van Lancker looks at Banyay and says, "The race starts here." On Sunday, this is where the riders will have nearly 100 miles of racing under their belts and where the final selections will begin. The Belgian director knows every turn and points out places where wrecks happened in previous editions of the 159-mile race, which was first run in 1892. Near the base of the Col du Maquisard just outside the original resort town of Spa, he points to a place where a truck once lost its brakes and smashed into a house.

Leaving Sprimont, the town that follows the famous La Redoute climb, Van Lancker points toward a gas station. "See that Q8? That's where I go." In 1990, that's the point where he attacked the Liège peloton, rode away, and won. "Even now, whenever I see a Q8," Van Lancker adds, "I think, 'Attack!'" Still trim and fit, Van Lancker also won the Amstel Gold Race in 1989 and stays tuned to the pulse of Belgian cycling through his job as a cycling coach at Belgian schools. Noting the big crowds even at midweek events like Flèche Wallonne, Brabantse Pijl, and Sheldenprijs, Van Lancker wonders aloud, "Doesn't anyone work?"

La Doyenne—as Liège-Bastogne-Liège is nicknamed because of its seniority among the classics—wraps relentlessly into the deep valleys and steep ridges of the mountainous Belgian Ardennes. This is especially true toward the end, where the climbs come with castrating regularity. Spinning through steep pine-clad hills on roads dappled with spring sunshine and dotted with bell-clanking cows, it's no wonder this is a popular vacation destination for Belgians escaping urban Brussels.

TOP Two days before the race, Christophe Le Mével pre-rides the Liège-Bastogne-Liège course in the Belgian Ardennes. RIGHT Peter Stetina, Ryder Hesjedal, Christophe Le Mével, Christian Vande Velde, and Dan Martin (left to right) getting an early taste of the Liège hills.

Christophe Le Mével helps a Belgian boy up one of
the climbs of Liège-Bastogne-Liège.

Passing through a hamlet tucked into the folds
of a deep Ardennes valley, a clot of kids charges out
of a yard, screaming *"Bidon! Bidon! Bidon!"* Vande
Velde tosses a bottle their way. Three kids scrap
over it like seagulls after a hamburger bun. In the
woods, pollen billows from trees in clouds. Back
arched and elbows bent, Hesjedal floats up the 12.2
percent grade of the Côte de Stockeu. He pulls far
ahead of his teammates, testing his fitness. Behind,
Martin winces. His damaged elbow makes it painful
to pull on his bike's bars. This is the climb where, in
the 2010 Tour de France, much of the field wiped
out when descending the damp and greasy road.
Van Lancker asks Hesjedal if he remembers. "I'll
never forget it," the Canadian responds.

Toward the end of the ride, as the team approaches the top of another climb, they pass a boy, about
11, cycling on the sidewalk. The boy bunny hops
onto the street and sprints to the Garmin-Cervélo
guys. Le Mével looks over with a smile and says,
"Allez, allez!" The lad hangs on for a hundred meters
or so, then begins to flag.

Le Mével sits up. When the boy catches him, the
Frenchman puts his hand on the small of the young-
ster's back and pushes him over the top. There,
Le Mével pulls a water bottle out of his cage and
hands it to him. Joyous with gratitude, the boy holds
up the bottle like a gift from heaven.

After the ride, the riders slip quickly into the
waiting bus. Before Banyay even has their bikes

Christophe Le Mével on the last of three ascents of La Flèche Wallonne's Mur de Huy. He placed ninth.

on top of our support car, the bus is gone. "That's a good thing about riders in Europe," the Californian says. "They don't dick around. Riders in America, they want to hang around and chat."

That night, after massages and dinner, roommates Vande Velde and Hesjedal lie in their Genk hotel beds. MTV's *The Real World* is on TV. "I love this show!" Vande Velde says, though it's unclear if those are words of adoration or dismissal. Hesjedal glances at the screen and emits a laconic "hmm." The two interact with the relaxed manner of longtime roommates, among whom much communication takes place without words. A two-liter water bottle sits on Vande Velde's nightstand, taken from the six-packs soigneurs leave in the hallways for the riders each night. With one eye on the shambolic proceedings on TV, Vande Velde's right hand sweeps across his Macintosh laptop touch pad and scrolls through a cycling Web site. Clothes spill out of the riders' luggage, and their shoes sit on the floor, awaiting the next day's battle in the Belgian Ardennes.

LIÈGE-BASTOGNE-LIÈGE HIDES A BRUTAL fist beneath a velvety green glove of forested hills. On this Sunday race morning in Genk, the sun is just rising over the lake outside the hotel dining room as Le Mével fills his breakfast plate with spaghetti. Martin, American Tom Danielson, Australian Cam Meyer, and the rest of the team eat bread, oatmeal, fruit, and muesli. Martin says when he was a junior, he thought he could eat more than usual before races, but now he just eats more on the road. "I learned my lesson," he says of his youthful efforts at pre-race gorging. Earlier, before any riders arrived, Morahan placed a basket of colored eggs on the table. "Something special for the boys," she says. Sighting the basket, Danielson pronounces, "Oh, it's Easter!" He is silent for a moment. "I miss my son." Vande Velde says his two daughters will be hunting Easter eggs at home.

The race is a bust for the team. Just 45 miles after the start in Liège, the field scampers up the Côte de Saint-Roche. Yellow flower fields paint the distant landscape. German hard man Jens Voigt of Leopard Trek is forcing the pace at the front, and all the Garmin-Cervélo riders are with the main bunch. Three little boys out for the day with their family from Luxembourg put up a chant directed at their compatriots Franck and Andy Schleck: "Allez Schleck! Allez Schleck! Allez Schleck!" One of the Schleck brothers spots them and tosses a bottle. Thunderstruck by this miracle, they boys clutch and dance around the bottle as if it were a maypole. Schoonaker exclaims, "This is crazy—I've never seen so many people here."

Fifty miles later the unstoppable Voigt is still throttling it as the attenuated field flows up through the sun-dappled woods shrouding the Côte de Wanne. Vande Velde and Hesjedal are right there, but Martin and Matt Wilson are off the back. Wilson packs it in at the next feed station. Martin's elbow is sapping his will. Reichlin says it's hard to do a race of this extreme difficulty "when your head isn't in it."

At the mile-and-a-half Mont-Theux climb, in a suburb outside Verviers 30 miles later, Le Mével and Hesjedal remain in the main group, where Andy and Franck Schleck are looking ominously comfortable, along with Belgian strongman Philippe Gilbert. The field is in tatters, and Vande Velde hangs on to its tail end. Danielson follows not long after. Thirty miles farther at the finish in Ans, a gritty Liège suburb, Gilbert shuts down the hapless Schlecks for his fourth win of the month.

Hesjedal lands the team's best result, 29th, 1:40 behind Gilbert. When Peter Stetina finishes, he is shiny with perspiration in the late-afternoon sun, lathery like a racehorse. Wiping his brow again and again, he says, "I can't get the sweat out of my eyes."

Christian Vande Velde's pre-race breakfast, Easter morning. OPPOSITE Ryder Hesjedal was the team's top-ranked rider at Liège-Bastogne-Liège, placing 29th.

ABOVE Dinner salads await the riders' arrival. RIGHT Team chefs Barbara and Chris Grealish prepare a curry dish on a camp stove in a North Lake Tahoe hotel parking lot.

out that eating in the hotels subjects riders to the whims of the hotel cooking staff, where the team has little to no control over ingredients. Add the prospect of 150 other riders—plus at least as many team staffers—coming in contact with serving utensils in a hotel buffet line, and there are health risks. A rider who picks up a virus can easily pass it on to teammates in the close confines of the bus, taking out the entire squad.

Vansummeren wanders down to the chilly parking lot a few minutes after 7:00. It was warm and sunny all of April back home in Belgium, and now California greets him with slate-gray skies and 30-degree air. He gestures at the clouds, which are threatening to spit snow, and says it's 23°C (73°F) back home in Lommel. "It's crazy." Vansummeren

has been to California before. He visited with his parents when he was 13. "We went to the place with the big trees" (Sequoia National Park).

Inside the bus, Hushovd sits next to Vansummeren, who is wearing compression socks. Sharing a table with Danielson and Zabriskie, they eat curry, salad, and beets with gusto. It's like a family camping trip.

THE NEXT MORNING THE BUS AND PARKING lot are blanketed in snow. The Tour of California organizers, AEG, made a Tahoe bet and lost. Instead of a brightly colored peloton streaming past the cerulean blue lake, May 15 at 6,225 feet delivers blue-black waters ripped by gusting winds and stinging snow squalls.

At the start line, tulips poke up through the snow. Fans wander, hugging themselves against the cold. With the riders staged behind them and dressed in gloves and face masks suitable for a December cyclocross race, Vaughters and other team directors get into a spirited discussion with the AEG brass about whether the race should proceed. AEG calls off the race minutes before its already delayed start. Some parts of the course are covered in slush so treacherous it sends an advance formation of photographers' motorcycles crashing to the icy road. Later, Vansummeren says he's happy the stage does not start. "I was glad that there was snow the first day. A 200-kilometer stage with those climbs, it would have killed me!"

It isn't just bad weather that pulls the plug on stage one. The previous week Wouter Weylandt died at the Tour of Italy—the same Weylandt who got tangled with his close friend Tyler Farrar a month ago at Scheldeprijs. Weylandt crashed on a Giro descent in northwest Italy and died of head injuries. The fresh memory of a young man's death in the prime of his life weighs on the start line debate.

Dan Martin thinks the fact that racing under these conditions is even being discussed shows both how little power the riders have and their lack of any sort of collectivized presence. "All the riders are like, 'Oh, I hope they don't make us race.'" Martin mocks, shaking his head in disgust. Then he scoffs, "How old are you? I mean, seriously! Let's just not race. Stand together, nobody wants to race, we don't

LEFT Alex Banyay prepares bikes for stage one of the Amgen Tour of California in North Lake Tahoe. BELOW Fans Tim Ackley, Chris Blancett, and Regina Molina (left to right) at the start of stage two in Nevada City.

Tom Danielson rolls out for the stage three start in the Sierra Nevada mountain foothills town of Auburn.

Regina Molina wait for the riders to come out. They clutch Garmin-Cervélo posters they are hoping have riders sign. These are superfans—especially of Dave Zabriskie. Blancett, who wears a red, white, and blue Dave Zabriskie Captain America T-shirt, says he likes all the American teams, but particularly this one because it fills an absence. "Lance is leaving," he says of Armstrong's retirement in early 2011. "So who am I going to love?"

When Hushovd rounds a corner onto Nevada City's Old West–style Main Street, he triggers a reaction in the assembled crowd. Then they recognize the tall guy next to him as the winner of Paris-Roubaix. It is as if a couple of rare, northern European cormorants flew way off their migratory route and alighted outside a birder's convention in this small Sierra Nevada foothills town. Vansummeren and Hushovd are a sensation.

Vansummeren rides in front of Hushovd on the mostly downhill race into California's capital city of Sacramento, protecting him from the winds blowing across the levees and rice fields of the Sacramento–San Joaquin River Delta. On the first of three laps around the domed capitol building, Hesjedal rails away at the front of the field to set up Hushovd for the sprint. The Norwegian lands a seventh place, where he also sits in the general classification.

The next day, after a relatively flat 122-mile stage through California's central valley, Hushovd places third. After the stage, both Vaughters and the team's director of communications, Marya Pongrace, who acts as an air traffic controller between journalists and the riders they want to land on, are unusually reserved. The following day reveals why. On Sunday, American rider Tyler

think it's safe." Then he points out the rub. "But then you've always got some guy who wants to take advantage of the situation: 'Oh, these guys don't want to race? I'm going to try and win today—try and make my name.'" That the riders are not always given a grown-up seat at the table is perpetuated by the fact that they act, in Martin's words, "a bit like schoolkids; there is always someone trying to get one over on someone else."

With snowy conditions persisting in the Sierras, the second stage start moves from the Squaw Valley ski area to Nevada City, a foothills mining town below the snow line. At the Garmin-Cervélo team bus, race spectators Tim Ackley, Chris Blancett, and

ABOVE Christian Vande Velde with his fans in Auburn. LEFT Johan Vansummeren meets the press in Nevada City.

Hamilton, now excommunicated from cycling for doping, is going on the American TV news show *60 Minutes* to claim that he saw Lance Armstrong using the banned blood-boosting drug EPO. Both Vande Velde and Zabriskie rode with Armstrong on the U.S. Postal team during the years Hamilton claims he saw Armstrong dope. Journalists are going to want to talk to them.

Throughout the remaining days of the Tour of California, Pongrace builds a wall around the riders. Tour of California officials also try to keep the race from getting hijacked by the Hamilton story. Post-stage press conferences are now prefaced with a request that journalists stick to the race, rather than ask about Hamilton's case.

At the start of the mountainous 82-mile stage four from Livermore to a summit finish on Sierra Road above the Silicon Valley, the riders observe a moment of silence for Wouter Weylandt. As announcer Dave Towle starts the race, Vande Velde makes the sign of the cross and pushes off. The stage's spectacular finish atop Sierra Road, 1,943 feet above San Jose, is a logistical challenge, because the only infrastructure on the remote mountaintop is a fence surrounding a cow pasture. There, Tour of California race director, Andrew Messick, stands beneath the finish banner, satisfied that in spite of snow in the Sierras and doping stories about to air

on TV, the stage is going smoothly. Garmin-Cervélo animates the race.

Away in a break, Hesjedal rides up the base of Sierra Road alone until he is caught by Team RadioShack riders Levi Leipheimer and Chris Horner. Horner, now 40, goes on to win the stage. Danielson shows promise, finishing fifth, seven seconds behind Tour de France contender Andy Schleck. Danielson's finish on the nearly 2-mile final climb augurs well for both his fitness and his chance of being selected for the Tour de France team later this summer. Talansky wins the best young rider jersey, while Hesjedal takes the day's most courageous rider award. The team also has four riders in the general classification top 10, with Danielson third, Vande Velde fourth, Hesjedal seventh, and Talansky in ninth.

Back in January, the team's aerodynamics expert and sports science manager, Robby Ketchell, told me that in terms of raw physical potential, "Tom Danielson can win the Tour de France." Ketchell knows Danielson's capabilities in particular detail because he took on Danielson's personal training program this year. After a January training ride with Ketchell in the Girona countryside, Danielson shared his power output numbers with Ketchell, but asked me not to look at them.

Ketchell says the secrecy stems from the fact that some riders don't want to be second-guessed in the court of public opinion. "At some point, you have to just draw the line and be like, this is what I work on, this is what I do," he says in explanation of Danielson's reluctance to reveal his early season power numbers. Danielson has long been considered one of America's great cycling talents. He has

OPPOSITE After observing a moment of silence for Wouter Weylandt, Christian Vande Velde makes the sign of the cross at the stage four start in Livermore. TOP RIGHT Tour of California organizer Andrew Messick atop Sierra Road in San Jose. BOTTOM RIGHT Ryder Hesjedal and Johan Vansummeren in rough Monterey County terrain.

a run on Mount Washington Hill Climb records in New Hampshire, plus overall wins at the Tours of Langkawi, Georgia, and Austria, as well as two Tour of Spain top 10s.

Wins at more prestigious stage races seem to elude him, however, keeping him out of the Tour de France team selections. With Ketchell helping him since the beginning of the year, this stage of the Tour of California suggests Danielson is synchronizing all the disparate mental, physical, and social pieces that collaborate to create success. Ketchell, 28, has earned Danielson's trust. That is not as easy as it sounds, especially with accomplished pros. There are a lot of people out there shilling cycling products who want to associate them with a pro rider for instant credibility. As a result, riders are guarded. "I

think every athlete at this level goes through that with different people," Ketchell explains. And that, Ketchell adds, "is the advantage of hiring staff on your cycling team. That's their job. They are not trying to take your name as the athlete and put it on their Web site so that they can build a business behind it."

The next day begins in Seaside, the heart of Monterey Steinbeck country. Martin attacks immediately. This is difficult riding terrain, with rough, handlebar-rattling roads and relentless climbing over changing gradients—the sort of lumpy, setigerous terrain that made this area ideal for the nearby Fort Ord Army infantry training camp. Describing Martin's at-the-front racing, Vaughters says, "He is rarely ever in the middle." From January training rides up Girona's Els Angles climb to today's 2.5-mile Laureles Grade, Vaughters says, Martin thinks "in terms of 'how can I win?'" Vaughters adds that Martin is sometimes boisterous and always confident. "But that's what it takes for him to believe in himself."

That doughty personality is on full display today. Martin attacks relentlessly, stretching the peloton like taffy before it has had even 10 minutes to warm up for the 135 miles of racing ahead. Back in the field, Hesjedal and Vansummeren are near the front. The Belgian stands and grimaces, summoning forces to get over the day's first climb.

At one point Martin clips off the tip of the race alone, and a single rider bridges up to him. When his

TOP Dan Martin attacks outside Seaside on stage five. LEFT With Andrew Talansky's best young rider white jersey visible through mustard flowers, the field covers a Monterey County back road.

companion does not pull through, Martin does not act out with dramatic arm flourishes, imploring his companion to share the load. He just attacks again, as dogged as the World War II infantrymen who humped 75-pound backpacks to bivouacs in these hills some 70 years ago. By the summit of Laureles Grade, Martin's efforts weed a selection of 11 riders that includes three-time world road champion Oscar Freire, riding with the Dutch Rabobank team.

Fifty miles into the race, the route heads east into the flat, crop-filled Salinas Valley. Nearly four minutes after Martin's break passes, the field arrives at the feed zone. Hushovd stops and gets off his bike.

His Tour of California is over. The world champion later explains that he is sick and feels empty.

As the riders summit the third and final king of the mountain point above Lake Nacimiento in San Luis Obispo County, Martin's break is still off the front 110 miles after making his initial push outside Seaside. While Martin, Freire, British rider Chris Froome, and Dutchman Maarten Tjallingii continue to cycle through their turns at the front of the break, the domestic-based riders do not—they are merely surviving.

The break is finally caught in the final 6-mile run-in to Paso Robles. Martin's chance at glory is

While Dan Martin is in a break off the front during stage five, the peloton streams through the vineyards of San Luis Obispo County.

TOP LEFT Dan Martin takes a feed from mechanic Eric Fostvedt. BELOW Dan Martin after the queen stage to Mount Baldy. BOTTOM LEFT Martin works with escapees Jeff Louder (BMC) and Christopher Froome (Sky). BOTTOM RIGHT Martin in Paso Robles with Alyssa Morahan.

snuffed, but he is satisfied. At the finish, his jersey is streaked with salt. Wearing black sunglasses with diamond decorations, soigneur Alyssa Morahan trots up to Martin and thrusts a cold bottle of water at him. He gratefully accepts it, drains it, and asks for a Coke. Morahan reaches into her cooler bag and extracts an icy red can. Martin is shattered. He struggles with the can, finally asking, "Can you please open it?"

A swig of Coke in his belly, Martin works up the energy to grin and proudly point out that he did the opposite of what Vaughters told him to do, which is presumably to ride more conservatively on this, the longest stage of the Tour of California. Why? "I felt really strong again today." Morahan points down the street and explains how to ride to the team hotel. Bleary with fatigue, Martin asks her to repeat the series of turns. He rides off in search of the hotel.

The following day at the start of the 15-mile time trial in Solvang, the Tyler Hamilton news is coming to a boil. Reporters hang around the team bus looking for a quote. The *Beyond the Peloton* crew films Emma Pooley warming up for a women's TT event. "You can't be here when the guys warm up," Pongrace tells them. She is firm, but not rude.

Zabriskie is targeting this stage as an opportunity to upset Leipheimer, who has won in Solvang three times previously. It's Pongrace's job to carve out a sanctuary for the riders to focus their minds in advance of the time trial, which is as much a mental as a physical test. A writer from the *Denver Post* talks to Vaughters about the Hamilton case then asks Pongrace when he can talk to the riders. He can't, she says. Chagrined, the writer calls someone on his cell phone and describes his discouraging

efforts at getting more information about Hamilton, who has announced that he will return his 2004 Athens Olympic Gold medal. Doping, not racing, is the story of the day.

In spite of the pall Hamilton casts over the proceedings for some, Vansummeren enjoys his first week in California since he was a teenager. In the time trial he climbs an oak-tree lined hill away from Solvang's quaint, Danish-themed center, and a fan cries, "This isn't Paris-Roubaix, but it's not bad!" A minute later a blue helmet, smooth as a cue ball, pops over the crest of the hill. Vansummeren's teammate Zabriskie squirts past like a spheroidal drop of mercury, limbs gathered in, eyes devouring the yellow center line unspooling in front of him.

TOP Alex Banyay prepares bikes for the Solvang time trial. BOTTOM Aerodynamic time trial wheels.

Dave Zabriskie rides out of Solvang on his way to victory in the 15-mile stage six time trial.

Half an hour later, Zabriskie crushes the time trial, laying down a time that eventually bests second-place Leipheimer by 26 seconds, and sets a new course record: 30:35.92. "I just did my own thing," Zabriskie says after the event. He also notes that cutting meat, eggs, and dairy out of his diet is making a difference on the bike. "I don't feel like I have superpowers or anything," the recently converted vegan notes. "I actually feel like the season is not weighing as heavy on me." In a languid cadence, reminiscent of Canadian comedian Norm MacDonald, Zabriskie adds, "That's what I think. A lot of it is what you think."

The following day, Saturday, May 21, news breaks that the UCI has sent Vaughters an arm-

twisting letter threatening to charge him for UCI-covered drug-testing costs if he does not publicly rescind the idea, floated earlier in the year, of a cycling league separate from the UCI. Ironically, it is later revealed that the UCI, which is responsible for drug testing at the Tour of California, conducted no blood tests during the entire event.

On the road, today is the race's queen stage that winds through Southern California's San Gabriel Mountains and finishes atop the 6,354-foot Mount Baldy ski area. Andrew Talansky and Ryder Hesjedal break away on the day's first climb up Mount Baldy Road. Passing sprawling, boulder-filled flood-control channels that cut through acres of stucco housing developments, they develop a rhythm with five break companions. Crossing the first king of the mountain point at 4,527 feet, their gap hovers around two minutes.

This part of California is usually brown with smog, with air so opaque many visitors to Hollywood and Disneyland never realize the San Gabriel Mountains exist. Today, however, is pellucid. The craggy mountains form a dazzling backdrop, as Hesjedal and Talansky climb past fire-blasted tree trunks and splashes of mountain flowers. A couple of hours later, team doctor Prentice Steffen waits on Glendora Ridge Road with an armful of water bottles. As Talansky and Hesjedal tick away the vertical feet toward the day's second king of the mountain

TOP Star and water carrier: In the San Gabriel mountains near Los Angeles, Johan Vansummeren takes on bottles for delivery to his teammates in the peloton. BOTTOM Ryder Hesjedal followed by George Hincapie and Andrew Talansky during their stage seven breakaway.

at 3,442 feet, Steffen hands a bottle first to Talansky then to Hesjedal. Talansky's outreached left hand hits the bottle with a soft plop, not a jarring whack. To cushion the blow, Steffen allows his arm to move along with Talansky's for a split second while making the handoff. He repeats with Hesjedal, who takes a swig then pours the rest of the water down his neck. Some 60 miles into the race, a motorcycle race referee in a black and white striped shirt holds up a timing board that shows a 1:15 gap on the field. Talansky labors smoothly, though his gasping mouth shows he is suffering.

One year ago, the 23-year-old rider was racing on these roads as a barely paid U.S. domestic pro at the San Dimas Stage race, where he won the Best Young Rider prize. Today he is in the big leagues, throwing down in hopes of getting three minutes out front, a gap that, if maintained to the finish, would make up both his and Hesjedal's time deficits on GC leader Leipheimer. "He's a good, strong-minded guy, and he's got some good natural talent," Vaughters notes, when explaining why he plucked the Floridian out of the U.S. domestic circuit. "He can become a rider that can win one-week stage races."

Not yet, though. Leipheimer's RadioShack team keeps the break on a short leash and catches Hesjedal and Talansky on the day's final climb through an evergreen forest to the Mount Baldy ski area finish. Danielson shows his continued strength, placing fourth on the steep finish and moving into a podium position. Pulling on a wind jacket in the finish ski area parking lot, Danielson is ebullient and shiny with sweat.

Morahan mops Danielson's face and hands him a soda, as his wife, Stephanie, watches with their 14-month-old son, Steve, in her arms. Danielson beams at the sight of ESPN reporter Bonnie Ford. He gives her a one-arm hug and enthuses about his day in the trade. "It was really, really hard. But I've got to tell you, there's nothing like having all those people on the side of the road. It is incredible," he says. Comparing racing in the United States to racing in Europe, Danielson enthuses that it's "fun" to be with his countrymen. The fans know him and "try to push you and not the Euro guys; where when you are in Italy or something they push the Italian guys and not you."

Without prompting Danielson adds, "There's been a lot of negative press the last couple of days, but we are all one big family, and we love each other." His solid finish today has him riding a wave of ardor for his profession. "Our sport is the greatest sport in the world, and people can write all they want about negative things in the sport, but what you saw today was the most beautiful thing in sport there is. Pure pain, suffering, skill, determination, fans." Ford asks him if pain is beautiful. "It's part of life," he responds without a pause. "Pain is part of life, and overcoming it and succeeding is succeeding in life."

As an ESPN writer, Ford covers a lot of sports in addition to cycling, including tennis and a passel of Olympic events. She is optimistic that up-and-coming riders like Talansky and Martin are the vanguard of a new crop of clean cycling heroes. And, on the eve of the day that pro cycling's biggest doping scandal is to be reinvigorated on national TV, she thinks the cultural acceptance of drugs in the sport has dramatically changed. In her view, the dysfunctional nature of the UCI and its historical intersection with doping stands as a barrier to continued

ABOVE Andrew Talansky grabs water from chief medical officer Prentice Steffen. OPPOSITE On their way to the finish atop Mount Baldy, Hesjedal and Talansky toil past fire-ravaged trees.

TOP LEFT Tom Danielson after placing fourth on Mount Baldy and moving into GC podium position. TOP RIGHT Andrew Talansky. ABOVE Danielson on Mount Baldy with son Steve.

progress. But, she says, many Olympic sports share these same issues, and in cycling "probably we are going to see a lot of action and reform on that front in the next couple of years."

THE FOLLOWING MORNING, A CLUTCH OF Christian Vande Velde fans, holding a sign that says, "Happy B-Day #18 Christian," wait in a parking lot behind an upscale shopping mall in Santa Clarita, a suburb on the far northern reaches of Los Angeles. The team bus pulls up 90 minutes before the final stage start. Vande Velde steps out with a look that is a mix of gratitude and embarrassment. A few min-

utes later, Vaughters drives up with Zabriskie in a fiery red Porsche. "It's Christian's birthday present!" someone says. But, not really.

A friend who runs a car company loaned the sports car to Vaughters. Sensing an opportunity, Vaughters makes a phone call. He hangs up, beckons to mechanics Withington and Banyay, and instructs them to put bike racks on the car. He just got approval to drive the Porsche as his team car in today's stage. It's signature Vaughters; a quirky, spur-of-the-moment move that fits his fondness for the unconventional. The car also becomes a subject of attention for fans and the race photographers; by the end of the day, photos of the Garmin-Cervélo Porsche are all over the Internet. Garmin-Cervélo is always looking for car sponsors. In Europe the team is still using last year's well-worn Skodas, while at the Tour of California they rent Subarus wrapped in team colors. I ask whether the Porsche is meant to help with bringing on a future car sponsor. "That's the idea," Vaughters responds.

Vaughters's girlfriend, Ashley Haussman, is also hanging out in the parking lot. She looks on as a photographer on deadline hurriedly poses Vande Velde

in front of the bus for a Chicago magazine cover. A certified sommelier, Haussman has an NYU master's degree in English and American literature and runs a wine shop and wine consulting business in Denver. Whether here or at Paris-Roubaix, she seems to observe the spectacle of her boyfriend's touring company of bike racers with the lighthouse-like circumspection of an academic presenting a paper on dinner parties in the novels of Virginia Woolf. Vaughters asked her to fly out for the race finale. "You need to get out here, now!" she recalls him telling her by phone. Though he does not show it in public, the unexpected attention related to Hamilton's scheduled confessions plus the UCI's latest effort at squelching his efforts to change the sport do bug Vaughters. "I think he needed some company," she says.

At stage end, the race does a series of laps around downtown Thousand Oaks and finishes as a bunch. There is no change to the overall results, and on the basis of Danielson's third, Vande Velde's fourth, and Hesjedal's 10th placings, Garmin-Cervélo tops the team competition. All the team riders share the $5,000 team prize. As the team steps onto the stage in front of a deep and raucous crowd of cycling fans, Vande Velde and Martin have mischief in their eyes. Something is about to happen.

Vande Velde opens his champagne magnum and turns the horsetail of spray on the two podium girls, defenseless in their slinky black dresses. Martin follows suit, while Vaughters drenches Hesjedal. Amid

TOP In Santa Clarita, Christian Vande Velde and Alex Banyay with the day's team car, a borrowed Porsche. BOTTOM Amgen Tour of California team victors.

Vansummeren (far left) celebrates his first return to California since a family vacation at 13.

the mayhem, Zabriskie opens his bottle with Yoda-like presence of mind and unleashes a fire hose of wine on the photographers and their $8,000 cameras. A full magnum slips from Martin's hands and bounces off the stage, rocketing champagne like an Old Faithful of California bubbly. Vansummeren raises his hands in the air like a wide-eyed 13-year-old bearing witness to the Sequoias again—in mute, smiling awe at the spectacle unfolding around him. It's a scene of unadulterated bliss. "We had it all planned out," the delighted Martin says of the attack on the hapless podium girls.

That evening, Martin relaxes at the hotel bar with Hesjedal and Vande Velde. Even though Hamilton is about to go on TV and spill his guts, no one in the buzzing hotel lounge seems interested in watching. At least on the outside, the riders are immersed in a different world. Asked about his first Tour of California, Martin says he is impressed by how many American fans knew him by name. "I don't want to pigeonhole it, but it's the way people are over here. They either love the sport or they just don't know about it. People who are fans here are just 150 percent into and know everything about it. It's an awesome way to be, whereas in Europe, it's taken for granted."

The fact that an Irishman at the beginning of his cycling career is so well recognized reminds Martin of the fact that he and his colleagues deliver a product, something of diversionary and cultural value to fans. "This is definitely an entertainment business," he explains. "And that's what a lot of people forget. We are here to entertain the fans." While he is visibly exhausted, Martin is confident that with the team win, three riders in the top ten, and riders at the front animating the race every day, his team has fulfilled its professional obligation.

Aggressive racing comes up earlier that day at the post-race press conference. Someone asks if the race shouldn't be more difficult and what can be done to improve it. After Danielson dismisses the notion that the race should get harder, Vaughters points out that in six years the Tour of California

has built a reputation and fan attendance that rivals that of European races with more than 100 years of tradition. The challenge, Vaughters adds, is how to maintain a certain allegiance to that European tradition while moving the Tour of California ahead in new ways. "Cycling is a traditional sport. It's got a lot of history. To remain true to that while trying to innovate the sport is exactly what AEG, Medalist, Amgen, that's what these guys are doing," he says, ticking off the names of the promoters and lead sponsor of the race. "Little by little, they are going to get there," he adds.

Andrew Messick is the man who is ultimately behind the growth of the Tour of California. The 47-year-old organized the first six Tours of California for sports investment and management company AEG. Messick believes the Tour of California's value is rising, and, as evidence, he cites the fact that mainstream media outlets wait to break doping stories during the event. In 2010, *The Wall Street Journal* waited for the Tour of California to publish Floyd Landis's doping confessions, while in 2011 the CBS television network does the same with Tyler Hamilton. "Last year, this guy from *L'Équipe* [the French sports newspaper that, in a different incarnation, founded the Tour de France in 1903] walked up to me right in the middle of the Floyd-Lance shit storm," Messick recalls, producing a weary smile. "And he said, 'Congratulations.' And I said, 'Well, thank you, what for?' And he said, 'They don't do this at the little races.'"

THE TOUR DE FRANCE

5

Dave Zabriskie steps into the courtyard of the Manoir de la Babacane hotel in Tiffauges, France. Blinking at the afternoon sunlight, Zabriskie walks into the square that fronts the hotel. All the archetypes of France are here: stone church, café with window dripping flowers, gaily painted wine shop, old man tapping across the plaza with baguette tucked under his arm. Zabriskie scans the square and walks to a stone post in front of the church. "I'm taking Yoda out," he explains. He sets a six-inch-tall figurine of the *Star Wars* hero on the post, extracts a cell phone from his pocket, and snaps a picture. Wordlessly, Zabriskie picks up Yoda and they stroll off together into the heart of the village.

Two days before its July 2 start in Vendée, a region that sits just under the French coast's beak-like projection into the Atlantic, the world's attention turns to the 98th running of the Tour de France. This is the race that matters, the one that delivers the best return for team sponsors and riders alike. As Tour of California organizer Andrew Messick puts it, "The economics of the sport, everywhere, is all about the Tour de France." The reason a sponsor

will underwrite a team to the tune of $5 million to $15 million is the exposure they get at the *Grande Boucle*, the big loop, as the Tour is known.

And yet, while the anticipation is high for an event that draws more viewers than any sporting spectacle save the Olympics and World Cup, the mundane persists. In the hotel's cozy sitting room lobby, bus driver Andrea Bisogno sits on a couch with a thick stack of receipts. He prepares an expense report from last month's Tour of Italy. "8,000 euros," he says—about $12,000. That includes toll roads and fuel at $1,000 a tank. Outside, British soigneur Gavin King mounts a rack on the grill of the mechanics' truck and hangs T-shirts and shorts to dry.

The next morning the team hosts a pre-race press conference in the biggest room in Tiffauges, the primary school library. Drug testers make an unannounced visit as the riders are preparing to walk to the press conference, so Hushovd, Farrar, Vande Velde, and Zabriskie filter in one at a time after their sampling duties. They sit at a row of tables beneath the word *Bibliothèque* stenciled on a wall above,

TOP LEFT Dave Zabriskie with Yoda in Tiffauges, France, the team's base during the first days of the Tour. BELOW Bib shorts dry in the Tiffauges sunshine. RIGHT Pre-Tour press conference in Tiffauges's school library.

each letter a different primary color. The rest of the Tour squad—David Millar, Julian Dean, Ramunas Navardauskas, Ryder Hesjedal, and Tom Danielson hang back at the hotel.

Paul Kimmage, an Irish journalist whose cycling oeuvre is an extended anti-doping jeremiad, asks Vaughters what he thinks of a recent comment by five-time Tour winner and cycling legend Eddy Merckx that a new UCI no-needle policy is foolish. Vaughters flatly responds that "Eddy is wrong" and explains how the team came to its no-IV stance decision through rehydration research. When Kimmage presses the riders for their thoughts on the issue, Farrar does not bite. "I'm still here," he says, by way of explanation that for him, the team offers empirical justification that the best way to recover from racing and training is through oral hydration, not needles.

The next day's official team presentation takes place in a theme park called Le Puy du Fou, within its full-scale recreation of a Roman coliseum that usually stages mock gladiator fights and chariot races. Think Las Vegas meets the History Channel meets the Olympic opening ceremonies.

People stand in both the aisles and the open windows along the top of the arena. The first team, French squad Europcar, enters on horse-drawn chariots. Acrobats form a human pyramid atop running horses, while actors in medieval dress parade through trailing pennants and spitting balls of flame As the team awaits its turn below the arena floor, the riders come across a stash of props. Hushovd puts on a black, long-haired wig and picks up a caveman club. "Thor, you've got to do it man, you've

Team introduction at Le Puy du Fou theme park in the Vendée region of western France.

got to do it," Vande Velde encourages. Grinning, Hushovd holds the club over his head and lets out a roar. Vaughters finds an alternative prop, a sledgehammer, and hands it to Hushovd. The rumble of the announcer echoes from above. When the stage rises from the bowels of the coliseum toward the sky, Hushovd stands smiling in the wig and waving Thor's hammer. On their knees below him, his eight teammates ululate in obeisance. The crowd roars with appreciation.

STAGE ONE OF THE TOUR DE FRANCE from the submerged Passage du Gois on France's Atlantic coast to Mont des Alouettes ends its 119-mile length with a 1.5-mile, 5 percent climb. Hushovd finishes third behind Philippe Gilbert and Cadel Evans. On the other side of the finish line, Hushovd slumps his face into his arms, which are crossed over his handlebars. Millar gently touches Hushovd's back. Photographers shove clattering, brick-sized cameras at the rainbow-jerseyed rider's face, while reporters shout questions. Acknowledging none of this, Hushovd finally lifts his head and pushes out of the bedlam.

The next day Vaughters is tense. While the riders warm up on trainers in a supermarket parking lot for the Les Essarts team time trial, he paces and obsessively checks his phone. Working with aerodynamics whiz Ketchell, Vaughters and the team have targeted this day since the Tour route was announced last October.

For spectators, the team time trial is the discipline where the team nature of bike racing is clear-

ABOVE Riders warm up for the team time trial in Les Essarts. LEFT With Hushovd wearing a wig and bearing Thor's Hammer, the team rises into the Puy du Fou coliseum on a stage lift.

est. Rather than being spread like scattered blue dots through the pointillist 200-rider peloton, the nine riders work together as a visually cogent collective. Should one rider make a mistake—overlap a wheel, perhaps—the entire orchestra hits the deck in a cacophony of carbon fiber, metal, and flesh. And since Cervélo does significant business in the triathlon market, winning this stage generates extra publicity among that sport's aerodynamic efficiency-focused buyers. Also, a win in the team trial means that not just one, but nine riders can add a Tour de France stage win to their résumés. When it comes to soliciting sponsors, Tour de France stage wins are the gold standard.

Vaughters stays busy placing ice water–soaked towels on the riders' shoulders. Their legs whir like eggbeaters. Digital clocks mounted on the side of the bus ensure they don't pull a Pedro Delgado, the Spanish rider who showed up 2:40 late for his time trial start at the 1989 Tour. At 2:45 p.m., Vaughters shouts, "Two more minutes!"

The team burns off sprinters Dean and Farrar over the first half of the twisting 14-mile course. Then they close by leaning on the forces of time trial specialists Millar and Zabriskie as well as young Lithuanian national champion Navardauskas. The team crosses the finish line with the best time of the day and follows Hushovd's polka-dot skin suit through a mob of fans waiting outside the riot fencing that keeps a modicum of calm for a few hundred yards after the finish. (Hushovd is in the climber's jersey because after stage one, the general classification leader, Philippe Gilbert, also leads the points and climbing competitions. In cases where the yellow jersey wearer also owns the green and polka

LEFT David Millar comforts Thor Hushovd after stage one to Mont des Alouettes, where Hushovd placed third. BELOW Ramunas Navardauskas at the front of the team time trial rotation in Les Essarts.

RIGHT The staff erupts when BMC fails to best Garmin-Cervélo's TTT time. BELOW In Les Essarts, Jonathan Vaughters celebrates his team's first-ever Tour de France stage win while soigneur John Murray (center) and physical therapist Matt Rabin (right) look on.

dot jerseys, those shirts are worn by riders next in the points lines beneath the leader; thus second-place Cadel Evans wears green, while third-place Hushovd wears the dots.) Hesjedal puts his hand on Navardauskas's back and says, "You were an engine."

Navardauskas, 23, is a phenomenon Vaughters found in plain sight. While he gave the Lithuanian the call to join the Tour team only 10 days before the race start, he had his eye on him long before. In 2010 Navardauskas won the under-23 version of Paris-Roubaix and placed fourth in the U23 Tour of Flanders. Yet pro teams were not waving contracts at him. There were two reasons for that, Vaughters explains. First, Navardauskas does not come from a cycling powerhouse. Though in the fourteenth century Lithuania was the largest country in Europe and in 1990 became the first republic to declare independence from the U.S.S.R., most would be challenged to locate the West Virginia–sized nation tucked between Poland, Finland, and the Baltic Sea. Second, says Vaughters, "He won too much. The Frenchies all thought he was doping."

So, Vaughters decided to test the rumors. First, he met Navardauskas: "Super nice kid." The down-to-earth, humble Lithuanian did not conform to the cheater mold. "This doesn't fit together," Vaughters recalls of his efforts to reconcile the 6 foot 3, 170-pound young man sitting in front of him with the doping rumors generated by his winning record. Next Vaughters gave his gut reaction an empirical test. Minutes after Navardauskas won a race, Vaughters called him without warning and put him on a plane to Girona, where the team tested his blood, urine, and power output within 12 hours of his victory. Vaughters repeated that process twice, each time coming to the same conclusion: "The objective data pointed to a completely clean rider that was just super talented and super strong." And when Vaughters looked at Navardauskas's power tests, he found results of "6 watts per kilogram—better than the guys we were sending to the Tour last year." So he hired him. Vaughters loves data, and "I went with that as opposed to the rumor and the bullshit."

With soapy shower water running out of the bottom of the bus, the staff and mechanics gather around a TV placed inside the luggage compartment. As they watch the remaining teams finish the TTT, mechanic Kris Withington puts his hand on his forehead, as if to hold in unbearable tension. Ketchell, the technical mastermind who dedicated most of his waking hours to this moment over the last year, pinches his chin with his left hand, holding his head up in a sort of state of suspended anticipation. When the last team on the road fails to beat the Garmin-Cervélo time, the staff erupts. Vaughters flies out of the bus with a howl and pogos from one embrace to another. Millar emerges and stretches his arms toward the sun. Slipstream has its first ever Tour stage win. And not only does the team win the day's stage, but Hushovd takes the yellow jersey.

Two hours after the team picks up Vaughters and holds him in a human rickshaw on the awards stage, all that remains in the parking lot is a Garmin van carrying a couple of VIPs, Ketchell, Fernandez, and three members of Tom Danielson's family: his wife, Stephanie, their toddler, Steve, and his mother-in-law, Christiane. The clang of workers tearing down barricades echoes in the background. An inflatable thunder stick blows across the lot.

Ketchell clutches two bouquets of flowers against the warm afternoon wind. Fernandez carries Hushovd's yellow Crédit Lyonnais lion—a fuzzy stuffed animal given to each stage winner—on his head like a pot of water. They squeeze into the van and disappear, leaving Danielson's family alone in the parking lot.

Stephanie says this day has been a long time coming. While Danielson has been telling the press that having a child has given him additional resolve, she says there is more to the story. Thinking back to all the hours motor-pacing her husband from their home in Boulder, Colorado, she says, "He's coming in with a clear mind."

TOP On July 4 in Redon, Tyler Farrar celebrates his stage win with a remembrance of Wouter Weylandt. BOTTOM The team time trial victory is a key moment for the team.

ABOVE Tom Danielson congratulates Farrar in Redon while Ryder Hesjedal looks for his teammates. RIGHT Julian Dean after Tyler Farrar's win in Redon.

seaside village of Olonne-Sur-Mer to Redon. The field captures the breakaway 6 miles from the finish. On the run-in it looks like another Mark Cavendish win is in the offing. But then, with less than 1 kilometer to go, Millar keeps Hushovd protected through a right-hand turn, then the yellow jersey barrels past a stunned Cavendish with Dean and Farrar in tow. Dean takes over from Hushovd and drops off Farrar 250 meters from the finish in Redon.

Farrar wins the team's second stage in two days. The manner in which Hushovd made it happen is unprecedented. This is the first time a rider wearing both the rainbow stripes of the road world champion and the yellow jersey has led out a teammate for a win in the last 500 meters of a Tour stage. At the finish, Farrar and his two lead-out men reenact the historic moment through a time-delayed doppelgänger; while Farrar coasts past the finish line in real-time, hands held aloft in the shape of a W, on a JumboTron behind them and on TVs around the planet, a time-delayed Farrar is still sprinting, hands on his bars, elbows out with escorts Dean and Hushovd peeling off to his right.

After the stage, Farrar says he won it for Weylandt. The sprinter from the state of Washington is the first American to win a Tour stage on July 4, his country's Independence Day. As of today the 27-year-old is also the second American to have won stages at all three grand tours—Dave Zabriskie being the first.

At the finish, Millar scrambles through a frenzy of journalists to Farrar. With a Colombian radio reporter providing a live account in machine-gun Spanish to listeners back home, Millar plants a kiss on Farrar's cheek. Vande Velde hugs Farrar and tells him it's a great way to celebrate the Fourth. New

Though Danielson turned pro in 2002, this is his first Tour. "He had proven that he was ready," Vaughters explains, referring to Danielson's impressive spring rides in California and the Tours of Romandie and Switzerland. "He showed stability. That's what you need for a three-week stage race." As for what changed in the previously fragile Danielson, Vaughters suspects that "he decided to finally stop worrying about what could go wrong and what did go wrong and start just riding his bike."

The day after the time trial win, Navardauskas and Zabriskie keep five breakaway riders within reach for much of the flat 123-mile stage from the

Zealander Dean is usually emotionless after races, a countenance of blank concentration. Today, however, a smile shows through road grime that covers his face in the patterns of a Maori tattoo.

The marketing return on Farrar's win rains down within hours. U.S. Senator John Kerry e-mails Vaughters his congratulations. Articles headlining Garmin-Cervélo pop up on media sites around the world. *Forbes*, CBS, ESPN, *The Washington Post*, *The Guardian*: the world's press is smitten with the story of an American winning on July 4, an American who suffered tragedy months earlier with the loss of his dear friend. The next day's *L'Équipe* headline reads, in English, "Farrar's Day" with a full-page photo of Farrar with his hands forming a W.

During the race's first week up France's windy west coast and into Brittany, Navardauskas spends

TOP Ramunas Navardauskas and the peloton ride through the village of St.-Germain-Lembron during stage nine. RIGHT The peloton passes through the Brittany village of Dol-de-Bretagne on stage six.

TOP Thor Hushovd digs deep on stage four in Mûr-de-Bretagne. MIDDLE Hushovd takes his seventh yellow jersey in Super-Besse Sancy. BOTTOM A fan reads about Hushovd in *L'Équipe*. OPPOSITE Entering the Massif Central in Albepierre-Bredons.

miles at the front trading monster pulls with Zabriskie. With about 10 miles remaining in stage four, Zabriskie locomotives with such force that the field strains into a long, single-file line. Even Millar struggles to stay on. Navardauskas and DZ's efforts pull back a breakaway and Hushovd preserves his GC lead for another day. Watching on TV, fans can't help but note that Slipstream's days of hanging on and hoping for opportunistic wins are over. Motivated by two wins and possession of the yellow jersey, the team animates the race.

In the team hotel after a crash-filled stage five to Cap Fréhel, where Hushovd places sixth on a seaside finish above the ragged coast of Brittany, Navardauskas says Vaughters's presence helps him at his first Tour. Compared with the local races he was doing only nine months ago, he is a wide-eyed immigrant plopped unexpectedly in the alien world of cycling's grandest spectacle. "Before the Tour I was afraid to come here," Navardauskas recounts in a tone of semi-stunned reverence. But, he says Vaughters told him, "Relax, everything will be OK."

Navardauskas recalls that when the riders were in the team bus in Les Essarts waiting to see if they would win, the weight of the moment did not fully register with him. For guys like Vande Velde and Millar, who have been trying for four years for this day, the significance of the time trial victory was much larger than what he could appreciate. Three days after the fact, however, "Only now it comes to me, like, oh, really we really did this. It's a big step."

From the time trial win to Farrar's stage to Hushovd's seven-day run in the yellow jersey, the one-week-old Tour de France is already a raging success for the team. It even brings hope to

Kimmage, the Irish writer and ex-pro whose pessimism about the sport's doping culture knows no limits. After retiring from the peloton in 1989, Kimmage published *A Rough Ride*, a book that describes the sport's chronic doping practices. It made him a cycling bête noire.

In the parking lot behind the team's Cap Fréhel hotel, Kimmage shoots videos of the mechanics changing cables on the riders' bikes. "I have to stop myself every day when I come to the race," Kimmage says. "I have to stop myself from going to the Garmin bus. I have to make myself go talk to other guys." And that's not just because Kimmage believes the Garmin-Cervélo riders are clean. "Why I like these people here is that they are all good, decent human beings. They are all good people, and I cannot say that about a lot of the other teams."

HUSHOVD DIGS DEEP AND HANGS ON to the yellow jersey by one second on the first mountain stage, the July 9 trek from Aigurande to Super-Besse Sancy in the remote, volcanic Puy de Dôme region. The next day, fans perched on cliffs above the July 10 climb through the Massif Central village of Albepierre-Bredons pass the time by reading a *L'Équipe* article titled "Hushovd the Climber." But the day does not end well; crashes take Zabriskie out of the race with a broken wrist, and the leader's jersey slips off Hushovd's back.

On July 14 the race confronts the Pyrenees. A road that looks like it was paved by a meandering snail traces deep green valleys to the stage-12 finish atop Luz-Ardiden. Orange-shirted fans on

ABOVE Luz-Ardiden. RIGHT Basque fans in the Pyrenees.

a rock promontory peer into the valley's profundity, looking for the approaching peloton. A kilometer from the 5,627-foot-high finish, Danielson passes through a parting sea of Basques waving fists, flags, and plastic boppers. From afar it looks like thousands of agitated cilia urging a blue egg up a 9-mile trench of humanity. On the second-to-last hairpin, a man holds a flare aloft while Basque flags wave around him. The lurid light traces the cheekbones of a gendarme. Danielson, his cheeks shiny and eyes lifted to the ski lift finish line above, rides through this tableau of semi-anarchic fervor into 11th place for the day. The graduate of Durango, Colorado's Fort Lewis College has also cracked the top 10 overall and sits ninth on the general classification.

Morahan gets Danielson off his bike, sets him down, pulls his arms through the sleeves of a jacket, and tucks a blue towel around his neck like a scarf. After racing over this climb, the category one Hourquette d'Ancizan and the fearsome, beyond-category 6,939-foot Col de Tourmalet, Danielson is reduced to following the soigneur's instructions; all individual volition has been left out on the road. Danielson's breath sends puffs of condensation in the high mountain air as he pulls on leggings. Finally he works up the energy to point out that he thinks he did OK in the first big day in the mountains, considering that he dropped his feed bag during the stage and fell short of energy as a result. "I stayed within my limits," he reports.

The next morning the UCI's drug testers pay the riders another visit at the Campanile Hotel outside Pau, rousing them with a knock on their doors. Hesjedal emerges from his room groggy and

disheveled with sleep. Team doctor Serge Niamke and the drug-testing technician escort him to the team bus. They go inside and shut the door. A few minutes later, Hesjedal steps down into the parking lot, squinting at the sun rising through the trees. The Canadian crashed on stage one, then again on stage seven when a rider ran into him and sent him somersaulting off his bike. With his back deeply bruised from this flip into a ditch, Hesjedal walks back to his room with a pained gait more befitting of Methuselah than a 30-year-old in his prime.

On paper, the day's stage from Pau doesn't look promising. With the 10-mile Col d'Aubisque poking up the middle of the stage profile like a circus tent, followed by 26 miles of descending into the Pyrenean foothills town of Lourdes, the stage is not selective enough for climbers like Danielson and Vande Velde. And it's too mountainous for sprinters like Farrar and Hushovd.

Or so it seems. With 60 miles remaining in the 97-mile stage, Hushovd gets in a 10-man break. At the bottom of the Aubisque, the Norwegian

Tom Danielson rides into ninth place overall on Luz Ardiden.

103

makes a thunderous attack and drops everyone in the break except Frenchmen David Moncoutié and Jérémy Roy.

By the top of the 5,607-foot climb, Roy and Moncoutié return the favor by dropping Hushovd and put nearly two minutes on him. But the world champion plummets through the serpentine descent like a one-man Norwegian bobsled team and catches Moncoutié on the descent. Moncoutié sits on Hushovd's wheel; he knows he can't beat him in a sprint, so there is no sense helping him catch his countryman, Roy.

At the finish in Lourdes, a big screen TV shows Hushovd's insane effort play out. Transfixed by the possibility of their man winning yet another stage, Viking hat–wearing Norwegians chant, "Thor, Thor, Thor," and a blond woman holds up a sign that reads, "Thor Hushovd the Ox." Their hero catches, then passes Roy. Is Hushovd, a sprinter, really about to win a Pyrenean stage? He rides across the finish line with arms aloft. Behind him, the crowd is a frenzied tableau, a Delacroix of waving pom-poms, lifted cameras, and out-of-body screaming that is almost religious in its tenor—an appropriate scene for Lourdes, a shrine visited each year by some 5 million Catholic pilgrims.

Hushovd's Garmin GPS shows his top speed on the descent from the Aubisque is 69.59 miles per hour. After the stage, Lionel Marie, the directeur sportif in the team car behind Hushovd, tells me he has "never done a descent like that. It's wonderful for the guys." When Hushovd had the gap down

Thor Hushovd wins stage 13 in Lourdes.

TOP LEFT Hushovd in the team car after his stage 13 win in Lourdes. ABOVE In the back seat of the team car, a bowl of food awaits. TOP RIGHT Fans crowd the car containing Hushovd in Lourdes.

to a minute and a half, Marie thought there was a chance he could catch Roy, but the director was by no means certain. His eyes shining with joy, Marie recounts how "on the last roundabout, I told him, 'Come on man, come on!' And, phewww . . . he did it!" He adds, "I told him to enjoy this moment, because, can you imagine, he won a stage in the Tour de France with the rainbow jersey. It's fantastic."

Long after all the team buses have left, Hushovd makes his way through a crowd of fans to a waiting team car. With the assistance of a Tour de France bouncer, he slips into the front seat, where he takes a moment to sign an autograph book for a boy in a polka dot climber's jersey. A plastic container of food with "Thor" written on the lid waits in

the backseat. Marie gets into the driver's seat, and Pongrace sits in the back, though she has a hard time shutting the door because as she gets in, a fan sticks his video camera through the door and won't pull it out. When police finally pry the videographer off the vehicle, Marie starts the engine and the crowd parts.

After a rest day spent eating Chipotle burritos and hanging out with sponsors and journalists at Château la Nerthe, a vineyard in the famous Rhône Valley appellation Châteauneuf-du-Pape, the 16th stage sends the riders off toward the Alps by threading them through tile-roofed Provence villages and miles of stony vineyards. Sixty miles into the 101-mile stage to Gap, Hushovd gets into a 10-man break with Hesjedal. It sticks. With 1 kilo-

LEFT The team digs into burritos on the first rest day in the Châteauneuf-du-Pape vineyard Château la Nerthe. ABOVE With Alyssa Morahan tending, David Millar shows the strain of the stage 14 finish atop the Plateau de Beille in the Pyrenees.

meter remaining, Hesjedal leads out Hushovd for yet another win, this time over fellow Norwegian Edvald Boasson Hagen. With Hesjedal placing third, the result—their fourth stage win—also puts Garmin-Cervélo firmly in the team GC lead.

With his team's candlepower burning bright, I ask Vaughters about a meeting he had after Roubaix with Tour owner ASO where he proposed that they enter a TV revenue-sharing program with the teams. Heroic rides like the one in Gap today bring eyeballs to TV, yet Hushovd does not see a cent of the TV revenue he is instrumental in generating. Vaughters says that ASO responded that the Tour de France does not need professional cyclists. "They just want a national race, with national teams," he says. Are they

bluffing? They may be, Vaughters says, but it doesn't really matter, because it is impossible to organize the riders and their teams into a bloc cohesive enough to call that bluff. While the teams might at first show a united front and agree not to show up at the Tour unless ASO sits at a bargaining table with them, Vaughters says that ASO will then work behind the scenes. "They can just pluck off a few French teams," he explains; remove a few bricks, and mistrust and doubt sends the structure crashing.

Sitting in the lobby of the team's truck-stop hotel off a Turin ring road the day after his Gap win, Hushovd says both riders and teams are feckless in the face of ASO power. Since turning pro in 2000 with the French Crédit Agricole team (where

When not at their restaurant in Catalonia, El Racó d'Urús, chefs Sean and Olga Fowler travel with the team in a mobile kitchen van and prepare all meals at the Tour and other major European races.

Vaughters was his teammate), Hushovd says pro cycling has changed the way it measures and tracks details. From aerodynamics to nutrition, he says the sport governs incremental performance factors far more proficiently than ever before. Yet his profession can't master its financial details, and that frustrates him.

Leaning forward and speaking passionately, the often retiring Hushovd says lack of television revenue-sharing with teams and riders is "our big issue." He points out that the riders' original goal in going along with the UCI-created ProTour system of top-level races and teams in 2006 was to create a framework within which they could act as a collective "that was stronger than the UCI, that was stronger than the ASO. That was stronger than everybody." But, he continues, ASO saw risk to their monopoly in this collectivization. "ASO said, especially to the French teams, if you support this new association, you are not invited to the Tour de France."

And from a sponsor's point of view, that is untenable, because "the Tour de France is what it's all about," Hushovd says. On this evening in Italy, Hushovd surveys the pro cycling landscape from its absolute summit: He wears the world champion's colors, he has just spent seven days in the yellow jersey, and, in a sport where one Tour de France victory makes a career, he has added three more Tour stage wins to his lifetime stash of 10. And yet, he's vexed by his powerlessness in the face of the UCI and ASO. "The riders, we are like nothing. We can decide nothing. We are the last to know what is happening.

"It annoys me the amount of money ASO makes," he continues. "They sit on everything." That

On stage 15 from Limoux to Montpellier, Ramunas Navardauskas dives through a corner in Abeilhan, a hamlet in southern France's Languedoc-Roussillon region.

said, he also knows that ASO is the only race organizer making money, pointing out that other races either lose money or just break even. When I sketch out how Marvin Miller organized baseball players in the 1960s, Hushovd says, "That's the thing we are missing. Someone who can organize. But, sorry to use the word, we need to have balls to stand behind it. And maybe we have to lose six months of racing. But nobody wants to lose one race. Something has to change," he adds.

Yet Hushovd is also circumspect about pro cyclists' role as the primary actors in an inter-national sporting theater whose money-making potential grows every year. First, he acknowledges that ASO is a superb race organizer with the world's most valuable stage. "They give us really nice races. They give us the Tour de France, the biggest window we can imagine." The Tour, he points out, is extremely well organized, has more spectators than any other event, and has the best TV coverage. "Everyone wants to be part of it," he concedes.

The other reality that gives him perspective is his financial situation relative to other world champions he knows in Norway. Hushovd says

On the day Thor Hushovd wins stage 16 in Gap, the field passes through Suze-la-Rousse in Provence.

top athletes at home who excel in sports like cross-country skiing have day jobs because their sport offers little or no income. Of cyclist wages, he says, "We earn poor money if you compare it to baseball, soccer, Formula One, tennis, golf. But if you compare it to swimming or orienteering, skiing,

we make good money. . . . It's not that we are at the bottom of the tree, we are in the middle."

It's evident Hushovd finds the business side of cycling tedious, agitating. Reforming the business is a headache he doesn't want. Indeed, he has an agent to deal with the numbers, to help him capitalize on a value that skyrockets during the Tour. Two weeks after the Tour ends, Hushovd announces that he is moving to another team in 2012. Vaughters has no hard feelings. "Thor wanted a three-year contract at a very high price figure," Vaughters explains. With a budget that is much smaller than that of many other teams, Slipstream cannot come up with the higher salary, so Hushovd moves on to a team with the money to pay him what his performances warrant.

Hushovd says that when he makes a mistake in a race or grows frustrated about the sport, talking to his two-year-old daughter calms him. "I just forget about everything, because I know that to have a daughter who is healthy, that's the most important thing in life. You lose a bike race, it's bad. But in the end, it's only sport."

His doting on kids extends beyond his family. At the start of his winning stage from Pau to Lourdes, fans, many of them Norwegian, gather around the bus. Hushovd takes time to sign autographs, largely ignoring bewhiskered adults and focusing on the outstretched hands of kids. After a TV interview with the Norwegian pro-turned-broadcaster Dag Otto Lauritzen, he returns to the bus and sits in the front row. A 10-year-old boy looks at him through the curtained doorway. Suddenly Hushovd reaches down and hands the child a water bottle. Astonished, the boy turns to his mom and beams.

Hushovd says he takes time for children because he remembers how small moments can profoundly affect a life trajectory. When he tosses a bottle to the crowd during a race, he says he always throws it to a kid because that bottle might

Stage 18 with Tom Danielson on his way to a ninth place finish on the Col du Galibier in the French Alps.

inspire them to race. "I prefer to give an autograph to a kid than a 60-year-old man. I know the kid will be more happy, and he will have this memory for the rest of his life."

TWO DAYS LATER, THE TOUR IS DONE. Danielson's ninth place overall nets the team its fourth top-10 Tour finish in as many starts. (Vande Velde placed fourth in 2008, then-Slipstream-rider Bradley Wiggins placed fourth in 2009, and Hesjedal took seventh in 2010.) The team won four

stages, spent seven days with the yellow jersey, and won the team prize awarded to the squad with the fastest cumulative time among its top three finishers every day. And of course there's Hushovd's recherché stage-two record of being the only rider in Tour history to wear the polka dot jersey without having won a single climbing point.

Standing in the midst of a crowd of family and friends a few steps from the water fountains at the base of the Champs-Élysées, the riders double-fist beer and champagne. While a smiling Hushovd pops open a bottle of champagne, Vaughters emerges from the bus and asks for everyone's attention. He has an award for the top-placing rider older than 35. He holds up a gray jersey with a cartoonish figure of a man bent over a cane and with one hand on his back and announces, "Congratulations, Christian Grandpa Velde!" Smiling sheepishly, Vande Velde steps forward, puts on the jersey, and says, "I've never been so humiliated."

At 10:00 that night the team and guests sit for dinner at a lustrous restaurant with a rooftop deck overlooking the Eiffel Tower. As waiters glide about delivering the first course of *gambas poêlées*, Vaughters takes the microphone. He says before the Tour he wrote down five goals on a piece of paper: Win the team time trial, have both Hushovd and Farrar win a stage, put a rider in the top 10 general classification, win the team general classification, and hold the yellow jersey.

"There is no way it will ever work out," he thought at the time. "It will stretch the team too thin. It's just not possible." And yet, he marvels, the team accomplished every one of them. He compliments the mechanics, soigneurs, directors Marie

OPPOSITE Ryder Hesjedal leads on the Champs-Élysées. LEFT Christian Vande Velde with his top-placing masters rider jersey in Paris.

and Fernandez, the medical staff, and the team chefs, Sean and Olga Fowler. Then he says of his riders, "I learned in this race that the best thing for me to do is to set an objective for these guys every day and give them a couple of ideas on how to do it. And then let them do it.

"They have been incredible in every way, shape, and form," he continues. "In the intelligence they have shown. In the perseverance that they've shown. The power of the collective they've shown. The bond they've shown. The cohesion that they've shown is unbelievable. I've had the easiest job in the world. All I have to do is sit back there [in the team car] and eat potato chips and worry a lot."

Tour de France team victors with cutout of Dave Zabriskie.

The Eiffel Tower comes alive with shimmering veils of white lights. Vande Velde takes the microphone. "From pipe dreams in 2003 for Jonathan to 2007 for a couple of us taking some serious risks coming to this team in the first place. From being the little engine that could to standing the whole effing team on the podium in Paris. It's been huge."

Grinning and with a beer in hand, Vande Velde adds, "This Tour, I'm sure it's been fun to watch for you guys, but this Tour *sucked*. It's been hard. It's been terrifying. It's been a lot of everything. But you know, it's been fruitful, and we've been on the giving end, so cheers to everybody. This has been awesome. I'll never forget it."

USA PRO CYCLING CHALLENGE   6

Tom Danielson and Christian Vande Velde sit in the first row of a two-level dais at USA Cycling's headquarters in Colorado Springs, Colorado. As photographers jostle for angles, Vande Velde tells the standing-room-only press conference he is excited to be at the inaugural USA Pro Cycling Challenge—here, in North America, rather than "in Europe out in the middle of nowhere at races no one has really heard of."

Vande Velde's words might raise eyebrows—there is a lot of middle of nowhere in Colorado's 104,100 square miles, and the first-year race is, by definition, unheard of—were it not for the people sitting next to him and Danielson. Namely, the entire Tour de France podium: Cadel Evans, Andy and Franck Schleck, plus Giro d'Italia winner Ivan Basso and Dutch hero Robert Gesink to boot. The governor of Colorado and the mayor of Colorado Springs are also up there with the race organizers.

Meanwhile, UCI president Pat McQuaid and USA Cycling president Steve Johnson sit in the first row of the audience, two seats away from Vaughters. TV announcers Phil Liggett and Paul Sherwen are a row behind. As the press conference begins, Europe's third grand tour, the Vuelta a España, is entering Spain's Sierra Nevada mountains some 5,000 miles to the east, and yet the potentates of global cycling—riders, governors, managers, and media—are gathered here in a nondescript office park outside Colorado Springs, bequeathing a weighty endorsement for a debut event.

The race is important to the team for reasons both practical and sentimental. North America is Garmin's largest market, and Colorado is where both Vaughters's and many of his riders' love for cycling was sired because it was the birthplace of the Coors Classic, a legendary stage race held in the state from 1980 to 1988. The team's roster is loaded with crowd-drawing North Americans. Along with Vande Velde and Danielson, Coloradan Peter Stetina and Tom Peterson from the state of Washington are here. Captain America Zabriskie is riding, as is Hesjedal. Brit Dan Lloyd is the lone Euro. New face Danny Summerhill caps the squad; he's a 22-year-old Denver local, whom Vaughters pulled up from his development team for a taste of

Dave Zabriskie threads the Garden of the Gods in Colorado Springs during the USA Pro Cycling Challenge prologue.

the big leagues as a *stagiaire*—a term for under-23 riders who ride in ProTour races as apprentices.

Walking back to his BMW with Danielson and Vande Velde after the press conference, Vaughters says he is jazzed to have this level of racing back in his home state. "I wouldn't be involved with cycling if it weren't for the Coors Classic," he notes. That race drew Tour de France winners Greg LeMond and Bernard Hinault. Since its demise,

however, bike-crazy Coloradans have suffered a 25-year drought when it comes to high-level pro cycling. Does the presence of the best riders in the world mean that the United States is entering what McQuaid calls "a golden age" of multinational cycling? "No," Vaughters replies matter-of-factly. The race needs 20 years of history before it can show it won't "turn into a mushroom cloud." While he's delighted the race is in Colorado, and though it brings back gauzy memories of being a boy following the Coors Classic, he's been in the sport too long to start banking hopes and building dreams on a first-year event.

A few feet away, Vande Velde leans on Vaughters's car and shouts, "C'mon! Let's go!" "I gotta go," Vaughters says, then adds: "The Coors Classic inspired me to start racing bikes. Without great events like this, young kids don't have anything to look at, to see and feel like, 'Oh, I want to be a part of *that*!'" Vende Velde wants to get back to the hotel and chill out before tomorrow's stage; he looks at us in exasperation as Vaughters continues, "If you put on a great event like this with top competition, there's people that are going to want to be part of it, and there are kids that are going to want to be part of it. And that's how you have the next great American champions."

The next day's 5.2-mile prologue starts in the Garden of the Gods, a nature reserve above Colorado Springs. Crowds stand atop soaring red sandstone rock structures. A woman pushing a baby stroller asks her husband, "Can you believe this is happening?" It's a promising prologue for the team: Vande Velde takes second on the day and Summerhill rides away with the best young rider jersey.

The first mountain stage finishes at Mount Crested Butte, a 9,380-foot high ski area in western Colorado. The setting is beautiful. Warm sun and wildflowers dress a ski town of posh condominiums and massive log homes that are quite a change from the area's rough-and-tumble nineteenth-century coal mining heritage. The layout of the town is vaguely reminiscent of Alpe d'Huez, with a wide main street curving past ski lifts and condo

towers and ending at a commercial area. Unlike the scene last month at the Tour, however, it's pretty calm here.

Vande Velde finishes fifth, 7 seconds after winner Levi Leipheimer. Danielson follows in 10th, 11 seconds back. A few hours later, the team shambles in ones and twos across the parking lot to a camper van where chefs Chris and Barbara Grealish have an al fresco dinner waiting beneath a pop-up tent. The scent of marinated tri-tip floats on a gentle mountain breeze. Workers packing up the finish expo area turn their heads toward the toothsome smells.

Zabriskie steers clear of the meat and piles his plate with rice and salad. Everyone else tucks into

The peloton on stage two from Gunnison to Aspen.

RIGHT Dan Lloyd, Tom Peterson, Dave Zabriskie, and Peter Stetina (left to right) dine al fresco in the Crested Butte ski resort parking lot. BELOW On stage two, Tom Peterson takes a water feed from Jonathan Vaughters, who has UCI president Pat McQuaid along for the ride.

the tri-tip. DZ pays attention to his food. "When we cook fish," Chris says, "he wants to know its provenance." Zabriskie rolled in 122nd today, 5:22 after Leipheimer. I ask how the day went. "Ahhhhh, you know. . . ." he says, his voice trailing off in a Zabriskiesque drawl that seems part boredom, part astonishment at the marvelous, preposterous planet he inhabits. He turns his eyes to his bowl of rice. "I'm not going to kid," he blurts. "It was fucking hard."

Robby Ketchell shows up and asks Stetina about the stage. The young Coloradan is bummed. He got gapped off on a turn in the valley before the final climb and is furious at himself for losing 44 seconds to Leipheimer. "It was like a crit turn," he tells Ketchell of the sharp right-hander. "I lost my pants."

Nearby, Justin McCarthy is hanging around with a fancy looking box with a Garmin logo on it. McCarthy does public relations for Garmin, and this evening he is going on Versus, the American sports TV channel, to talk about the Vector, a new Garmin pedal that provides power output readings. Team sponsorship is getting Garmin an unexpected Vector TV ad. Seeing Garmin products like this in use at big races also "adds new meaning for our engineers back home," McCarthy says. As an example, he says during the Tour, employees are following the stage finishes, even those who are not cyclists. "When guys cross the finish line and you see photos of the products that these guys have been working on for years," it gives employees a singular sense of engagement and pride.

The next day crowds press in on the peloton as it crosses 12,095-foot Independence Pass, the second 12,000-plus climb of the day. A howling white-gloved man with a Mardi Gras mask and purple and green jester hat leans within inches of Danielson and Vande Velde. Ten yards farther down the raving tunnel of humanity, another man offers riders a tub of orange cheese ball snacks.

Between the climbs on the 130-mile stage, Zabriskie, Stetina, and Peterson clamp on to Leipheimer's wheel to keep Vande Velde within striking distance of the race leader. Behind the blue and black Garmin-Cervélo train trails a thread of orange and blue Rabobank riders, and then the field ravels into a mass of lower-profile European and domestic teams. It's a colorful manifestation of the pro cycling pecking order. The long climb to Independence Pass is reminiscent of the Pyrenees, with vast valleys, mountain lakes, and pine-covered hills. Only here, the landscape is not scribed by humans—it is void of stone villages and lonely mountain chapels.

Vaughters stops his team car at the feed zone, and his passenger, Pat McQuaid, who is along for a ride throughout the stage, gets out and takes a discreet leak in a clump of bushes. Because Vaughters and McQuaid have not been on best of terms, Vaughters says having the other man ride along was a spur-of-the-moment idea that came to him when he saw McQuaid at the stage start. Vaughters says the UCI president was somewhat surprised by the invitation, but graciously accepted. "You can attract more flies with honey than vinegar," Vaughters notes, grinning.

The 12,000-foot altitude seemed to neutralize the force of Europe's best climbers.

The day isn't entirely sweet for McQuaid. Early in the race, a group of riders crashes on a cattle guard. One is seriously injured, and during the stage that rider's director, Canadian former pro Steve Bauer, drives alongside the Garmin-Cervélo car, rolls down his window and excoriates McQuaid for his refusal to allow riders to use race radios. Bauer is no lightweight; he raced the Tour de France 11 times and placed fourth in 1988. Having spent more than two weeks in the yellow jersey during those years, he is a respected voice in the cycling cosmos. Later Vaughters tells me that while McQuaid acknowledged Bauer's criticism, the Irishman said the solution isn't race radios. Instead, McQuaid remarked that race organizers need to do a better job covering road hazards.

On the rainy finish in Aspen, Danielson gets away on the final 20-mile descent with fellow Americans George Hincapie and Tejay van Garderen and finishes 45 seconds in advance of the field. Though it is raining and the riders are shivering, Danielson poses for photos with fans. Soigneur Josep Colomer spies Stetina, cries, "There you are!" and mops the muck off his face with a towel. Stetina is in much better spirits than he was yesterday.

After the stage, the Grealishes pull their cooking van to the sprawling Aspen vacation home of team fan John Bucksbaum and prepare dinner. As Chris juices piles of beets in the kitchen, Bucksbaum tells me about his fascination with cycling. When not running real estate interests from his primary home in Chicago, 55-year-old Bucksbaum says he rides "15 to 20 hours a week" in the mountains and valleys surrounding Aspen. He stays in touch with fellow Chicagoan Vande Velde throughout the

BELOW Chris Grealish prepares beet juice for the team's Aspen dinner. RIGHT Afternoon thunderstorms build as the field approaches Aspen.

Tom Danielson behind race leader Levi Leipheimer (in yellow), followed by Tour de France winner Cadel Evans (BMC).

year and, though he is also a board member for the U.S. Ski Team, he lives and breathes cycling. As we talk, he pecks out a phone message to his cycling coach. He describes a sleep-monitoring apparatus he wears to help ensure he properly recovers from his long Rocky Mountain rides. He's been to 14 Tours de France and has supported cycling and ski-

ing programs since the 1980s. "The year wouldn't be complete without it," he says of his annual trips to France.

At 7:30 that evening the riders arrive and promptly queue at a long wooden table, heavy with platters bearing steaks, legumes, and salads. As the riders load up their plates, the sky above Aspen's green ski runs fills with alpenglow. Too tired for boisterous conversation, the riders quietly wander to tables on the Bucksbaums' wildflower-bedecked patio. Danny Summerhill tells a story of going to cyclocross worlds and ending up in a room with a heart-shaped bed with his roommate. Vaughters and team communications director Marya Pongrace discuss a request from a cycling magazine reporter who wants to write a piece on Danielson's bike, which uses technology that has not been formally announced to the public.

With a 130-mile stage in their legs, the riders are ready for bed as soon as dinner is done. They first gather for a group photo with their hosts, then pile into the bus and disappear to their team hotel.

THE STAGE THREE TIME TRIAL IN VAIL IS AS close to a Tour de France–style start as America has probably ever seen. Vail, an überexclusive ski area, where condominiums routinely sell for $2 million, has the cozy, pedestrian-friendly feel of a French mountain village, but with the glossy sheen and manicured orderliness that comes with being the playground of the world's aristocracy.

About a mile from the start, Geoff Brown gathers his mechanics around a whiteboard on the mechanics' trailer. The board lists each rider's start time. A team car takes each rider to the start, and the board details which car takes which rider

LEFT Fans on Independence Pass. ABOVE Ryder Hesjedal and the peloton pass aspen groves.

RIGHT In Vail, Robby Ketchell quenches a dog's thirst while Geoff Brown adjusts Dave Zabriskie's bike on a trainer; bus driver Kevin Galos looks on. BELOW Christian Vande Velde's Vail time trial time came up 0.53 seconds slower than Levi Leipheimer's.

and when. Zabriskie emerges from the bus with a sleepy gait. His red, white, and blue Captain America skinsuit is peeled to his waist. He asks Brown to place his trainer-mounted bike at the far end of the bus, facing away from the ogling crowd. "Away from all this stuff," he says, waving his hand in the general direction of the curious crowd. The gesture is not mean-spirited, just his way of saying he wants to concentrate. A spectator asks DZ if he will pose for a photo with his son. Zabriskie complies. "What do you say?" the boy's dad asks him. "Thank you, Captain America," the child whispers.

Ten minutes into his warm-up, Zabriskie pulls headphones from his ears and signals to the mechanics. He wants to move. As Summerhill observes from an open bus window, Brown migrates the bike and trainer to another pop-up tent. A gray-haired man with muscled calves and knee-length shorts looks on from the edge of the tent. His white dog pants on the end of a leash. Robby Ketchell fetches a cut-off water bottle, sets it on the ground, and fills it with water. Watching the dog slurp, Zabriskie gets on his bike and starts pedaling. In front of him ski runs plummet like grass avalanches from Vail's 8,000-foot peaks.

At the end of the day, Zabriskie places seventh in the 10-mile uphill race against the clock with a time of 26:46:50. Vande Velde's 25:47:66 time is 0.53 seconds shy of Levi Leipheimer's winning time. Leipheimer moves into first place overall. It's a painful loss for Vande Velde, who falls 11 seconds behind the RadioShack rider after Leipheimer collects a 10-second time bonus. Despite having caught a stomach bug the night before and hardly sleeping, Tom Danielson rallies and places fourth for the day and also fourth on GC.

That night Zabriskie stands beneath the imposingly timbered porte-cochere of the Vail Marriott, waiting for a shuttle to take him and the rest of the team to dinner. Zabriskie is something of a cipher. He doesn't say much, and when he does speak, his voice has a tendency to trail off, as if halfway through each sentence he becomes aware of the absurdity of trying to contain an unruly world within the confines of language. Within the span of a phrase, he can also go from an air of wry detachment to intense engagement.

Zabriskie owns a company, DZ Nuts, which is also a Garmin-Cervélo team sponsor. DZ Nuts makes skin care creams for cyclists—chamois creams, shaving creams, and warm-up embrocations. "It was a little bit of a joke at first," Zabriskie recalls of how the company got its start. Other pro cyclists were introducing their own coffee brands, and that inspired him to do something irreverently different. Yet his product has a serious purpose, especially for a pro cyclist whose success correlates with hours on the bike. "I had always had issues with saddle sores," Zabriskie says. Through cycling connections in Salt Lake City, where Zabriskie used to live, he found a chemist, and the company was born. "It's been making history ever since," Zabriskie says, producing a sideways smile.

Today he sponsors the team by supplying them with his products. Outside of his business relationship with Garmin-Cervélo as a rider and

Vande Velde, chagrined on the Vail podium.

Riding here with Tom Danielson (left), stagiaire Danny Summerhill won an invite to Colorado with his bike-handling skills.

sponsor, Zabriskie says he "does not obsess" about the business of professional cycling. Then, half seriously he blurts out, "Andy Rihs should just buy the sport." Rihs is a Swiss businessman who bank-rolls BMC, the team that won the 2011 Tour de France with Cadel Evans and that is now hiring some of the costliest riders in cycling, including Hushovd and Belgian superstar Philippe Gilbert. "That's really how the sport survives," Zabriskie notes. "People like it, and they give it money." Zabriskie says his company is doing well, then jests, "We are going public soon; we are going to have Andy Rihs buy us."

Zabriskie turned pro a decade ago and says he has not seen the business side of the sport change dramatically over his career. However, he finds it interesting that "people are all pissed about these radios." He won't venture a guess as to why race radios brought riders together, at least temporarily. But he does not see an overarching rider's union taking shape. Instead, he feels riders are better off binding together to create small unions to repre-sent their interests within each team. He suddenly lets out an "Arghhhh" and shrugs his shoulders in an expression of the futility of the discussion. "You are never going to have a full-scale union that represents everyone. We have too many different nations, too many different languages, too many different mind-sets." And, frankly, the lack of rider cohesion doesn't bother him, because he sees pro cycling's dilemmas in relative terms. "There are so many other big prob-lems in the world that that's a comical problem."

UCI rules state that after August 1, pro teams can invite up to three under-23-year-old riders to join their teams. It's a way to bring young trainees, stagiaires, into the fold. After Zabriskie and the team return from dinner, I sit down with Summerhill, the 22-year-old rider that Vaughters brought up from its U23 development squad for this race. He is a U.S. under-23 cyclocross national champion, and that experience shows in how he handles his bike on rough, muddy roads. "He's the most Belgian rider from Colorado I've seen," Vaughters says, a refer-ence to that country's many great classics riders. He "has the instincts of a Belgian" and even "sits on the bike like a Belgian."

Summerhill has grown up entirely within the fold of Vaughters's program and is one of the younger generation of riders for whom doping has never been part of their world. "The idea of it alone is scary," he says of performance-enhancing drugs. Considering the years of work that have gone into building the team and its clean image, Summerhill shakes his head at the thought of how much damage doping could do. "If you were one of those cheaters, how could you look at yourself and know what you could potentially be doing to all these people who have put their blood, sweat, and tears into making this team?"

Summerhill's mother, Fran, recalls that when her son got the text telling him he was on the team for this race in his home state, he was "shocked, surprised, and thrilled." He got his first bike when he was four, she recollects. "He managed about two circuits around the driveway, fell off, didn't like the training wheels and took them off. From that point we just encouraged it," she says, her accent betraying her upbringing in Yorkshire, England. As a kid he would go out for two hours at a time practicing wheelies. At 16 he began racing with the 5280 squad, the first team Vaughters formed, which eventually grew into Garmin-Cervélo.

From a mother's point of view, Fran says Vaughters has had a positive influence on the sport. She cites his continuing support for the U23 team and juniors, despite the financial strain of supporting Slipstream's pro programs. And she feels Slipstream's anti-doping policy has changed the sport to a degree where she is comfortable with her son choosing it as a career. "I'm glad it's now and not even five years ago," she says of her son's introduction to ProTour level cycling. "He's never, ever run across drugs anywhere. Never seen it. And I'm pretty confident that the sport is slowly but surely getting a handle on it."

LEFT Danny Summerhill and fans in Denver. BELOW Christian Vande Velde before stage five from Steamboat Springs.

TWO DAYS LATER, THE RIDERS MASS AT another ski area, Steamboat Springs. On a day of what skiers call bluebird skies, Vande Velde signs autographs at the bus. Behind him, green ski runs plummet down Steamboat's mountain. Though he sits in an agonizing second place because of his half-second shortfall to Leipheimer in the Vail time trial, Vande Velde is smiling. "Do you guys ride bikes?" he asks a pair of boys. "Yeah! A LOT!" one responds.

Heading out of Steamboat, Tom Peterson gets away in a break with Italian Ivan Basso, Dutchman Laurens Ten Dam, and Tour de France second-place finisher Andy Schleck. The foursome labors smoothly all day, building a nearly five-minute lead as they pass boat-filled mountain lakes, snow-capped peaks, and lush valleys. But it's for naught, as Peterson and company are caught 300 meters from the finish line in Breckenridge, where thick crowds push up against the barriers for nearly 2 miles coming into town. The roar is deafening. It's no hyperbole to say that with each passing day, the crowds at the race become more and more like those at the Tour de France.

Indeed, the next day, after a relatively ceremonial ride to the race finish in Denver, Colorado, that sees Vande Velde place second overall and the team take the team competition prize, Colorado governor John Hickenlooper says, "This is our Tour de France." The most immediate and direct benefit of hosting the race, Hickenlooper tells me when I catch up with him behind the stage, "is people coming here and spending money." However, the indirect

OPPOSITE Departing Steamboat Mountain ski area. ABOVE Danny Summerhill just misses a podium spot on the final stage in Denver. LEFT Colorado's Peter Stetina watches the scene from the team bus.

Tom Peterson in a daylong break on stage five.

benefit is "the 20 million people around the world looking at the most beautiful parts of Colorado and hearing about local businesses and sponsors and thinking, 'Wow, I could open an office there.'"

After the race, the state reports that the event was televised for 25 hours and aired in 161 coun-tries. Of the estimated one million spectators, 22 percent traveled from other states, and the organiz-ers calculate that the race generated $83.5 million worth of spending.

Hickenlooper, who rode the time trial course in Vail in a charity event before stage three, bought his first bike in 1971, an Italian Frejus, popular with racing cyclists at the time. "The *Breaking Away* era," he says, in reference to the 1979 film of the same name. When he was 23, he spent a day riding 130 miles from Vermont to the shores of New Hampshire's Squam Lake (where the movie *On Golden Pond* was filmed). The memory seems to momentarily take the governor to a place far from our location in the swirling post-race commotion. It is one of those seminal, sustaining events that make a cyclist for life. "You start at six in the morning, stop and have a nice lunch, have a little nap and relax, and then just ride again." Looking out across the sea of race fans, he says, "It made me feel so . . . so *alive*."

The governor's heartfelt endorsement of cycling as an activity that both keeps him healthy today and furnishes his past with rich memories serves as a kind of perpetual motion machine; the love for cycling is a passion that does not easily wear out, and when experienced by people in high places, it can pave the way for complicated, public resource-intensive events like the USA Pro Cycling Challenge.

The field strings out through the vast spaces of Colorado.

After the riders celebrate their team victory with a champagne battle on the podium and Vande Velde poses on the second-place podium step, they filter back to the bus in front of the domed Colorado statehouse. Zabriskie, Lloyd, Hesjedal, and Summerhill fulfill a never-ending stream of autograph requests. Summerhill drapes his arm around his mom's shoulders and poses for photos with her, his girlfriend, and three of her friends. One holds a sign reading, "I love Spandex and Danny Summerhill!" A box of Chipotle burritos and a cooler of beer show up. Eating one of the bomb-sized burritos and drinking a Colorado microbrew, Garmin's Jon Cassat is startled by how Denver locals responded throughout the day when they found out he is from Garmin. "They kept thanking me for sponsoring the team."

A COUPLE OF WEEKS AFTER THE RACE, Christian Vande Velde is at home in Chicago. The season is nearly over for the 35-year-old veteran, and he's taking a break from yard-care duties on his seven acres of land. "I've been in the Bush Hog all day ripping up my yard," he says. After nine months on the road or living in Girona, he enjoys the domestic duties. "It's fun for me because I never get to do it during the year." Laughing, he adds, "I get to actually act like a man for a little bit!"

I ask how he is managing the half-second loss to Leipheimer in Colorado. "Oh, I'm still dealing with it," he says, chuckling uneasily. "It's not easy to deal with, that's for sure." Like Vaughters, Vande Velde as a kid was inspired by the stars at the Coors Classic, and those memories of watching American greats

like Davis Phinney and Andy Hampsten make his second-place finish especially poignant. "When I look at the kids, I wonder, do those kids view me the same way as I viewed the 7-Eleven team and Andy and Davis and Ron Kiefel and all those guys? It kind of freaks me out." By not finding an extra 0.53 seconds of time on his way up Vail Pass, Vande Velde implies that he somehow let down kids like those at the stage start in Steamboat Springs. "I'm not going to be the name that people remember; it's going to be Levi. He's got the record and half a second.

OPPOSITE Englishman Dan Lloyd, the squad's only European in Colorado. ABOVE Christian Vande Velde grabs lunch during 106-mile stage five.

That's what I think of, and that's hard to swallow." But Vande Velde already has a strategy for dealing with it: channeling his disappointment into a better future. "I've got to man up and go up it even faster next year."

Joining the neophyte Slipstream team was an audacious, even reckless decision for Vande Velde in 2008. He had an established record at the time, having raced his first grand tour at the Vuelta in 1998, and he supported Lance Armstrong during the Texan's 1999 and 2001 Tour de France wins, all on the U.S. Postal squad. That experience could have secured a position with an established team, yet Vande Velde chose the Slipstream offer. "I was scared," he says of his decision at the time. "I thought I made a big mistake after the first training camp."

Today, he says the choice was the right one because it opened up unexpected opportunities. "We were like this little Bad News Bears team who pulled up a lot of juniors, and now we just won the best team classification at the Tour de France. Saying that in 2006 I would have told you you were smoking crack." Vande Velde says he also looks at the decision with satisfaction because its repercussions go beyond his own career. "One of the things I'm most proud of is that I think we had a big part in changing to a clean sport as a whole." He mentions that he was one of the first athletes to document and publish his blood and urine test results. "Those kind of things I'm very proud of."

Coming full circle from his days watching the Coors Classic as a teenager to racing on the same Colorado roads as Hampsten and Kiefel, Vande Velde is bullish on the future of the sport in the United States. He explains that the block of North

American racing that follows the Tour de France—the Tour of Utah, the new USA Pro Cycling Challenge in Colorado, and the Grand Prix Cycliste de Québec and Montréal—relieves fans' post-Tour hangover. Rather than being let down by the end of racing, North Americans can watch the Tour riders in person at home. "People are coming from all sides of the country to watch the tour of Colorado; that's great," Vande Velde observes. "The more days of racing on a massive scale like the tour of Colorado and California, the better cycling will be."

And by *better*, Vande Velde means funded in a larger and steadier fashion, owing to interest from global companies, "the big breadwinners, the Fortune 500 companies." The growing interest from both North American fans on the ground and larger multinationals like Garmin, along with the abandonment of doping, are the biggest changes Vande Velde has seen over his career. His father-in-law is a case in point.

When Vande Velde started dating his wife, Leah, her father did not know much about pro cycling. Before the couple married in 2002, Vande Velde says her dad was "100 percent skeptical" about Vande Velde's vocation. He remembers "horrible" discussions with his fiancée's father, who was concerned about the young man wanting to tie his daughter to his two-wheeled destiny. At the time, Vande Velde was drawing a steady paycheck riding for the U.S. Postal team, yet his future father-in-law "asked me

OPPOSITE Garmin-Cervélo forms an echelon behind race leading Team RadioShack. TOP RIGHT Ryder Hesjedal. BOTTOM RIGHT Tom Peterson labors with breakaway companion Laurens Ten Dam.

what I was going to do for a living when I grew up— 'When are you going to get a real job?'"

Today, Vande Velde says he is more widely recognized and identified as a professional cyclist in the United States than he was during the days of his father-in-law's cross-examinations. He feels the fact that more people know about him and his sport is indicative of the growth of cycling as a legitimate entertainment performance in the United States. "Now it's playing in the bar on NBC and in prime time like it was in Colorado." As for his father-in-law, the painful interrogations are over; today he "is one of my biggest fans and doesn't get anything done at work because he's always watching cycling."

When Vande Velde was a teenager in the United States, his sport was still jettisoning its repute as a remote, oddball pastime for eccentrics. Think Dave Stoller shaving his legs and singing Italian arias in the movie *Breaking Away*. As Stoller's neighbor describes him from her vantage point on the porch, "He was as normal as pumpkin pie, and now look at him." Today, Vande Velde feels races like the one he almost won in Colorado are evidence cycling is ordinary. "Now you see guys who do mainstream sports and movie stars all riding their bikes and not ashamed of it by any means. At the end of the day, people are just realizing what it is. It's a cool sport. It's like X-games mixed with marathon."

OPPOSITE Fans rally Andy Schleck, Tom Peterson, and Ivan Basso shortly before they are caught in Breckenridge. LEFT Dave Zabriskie on the final stage circuits in Denver.

TOP Dan Martin wins stage nine atop La Covatilla ski mountain. ABOVE The Vuelta enters northwest Spain. RIGHT On stage 11, Dan Martin and Chris Anker Sörensen approach Galicia's Manzaneda ski station finish.

I think that's hypocritical. I think that's not fair. You always said fairness is a big value on this team.'" In retrospect, Vaughters feels his decision to send Peter Stetina instead of Bobridge to the Giro was the right one. He says he would do it again because it is fair to the collective enterprise.

While Internet cycling hangouts are loud with chatter about Hushovd's nonselection, Verin, Spain, is quiet on August 30, especially compared with the roar of downtown Denver two days earlier. This Tuesday is the first rest day in the 21-stage Vuelta, and wind rustles through the vineyards on the hills above the village in Spain's enchantingly green, remote northwestern province of Galicia. Though stage 11 starts here tomorrow, only one man sits at a table outside a bar on the main street. Except for two more men erecting rigging for the start line, there is no commotion, no clots of excited cycling fans riding through town, no window paintings celebrating the race like you find at the Tour de France.

Apart from Dan Martin winning stage nine at the La Covatilla ski area in the Sierra de Béjar west of Madrid on August 26, the Vuelta is not going easy on the team. Climber Christophe Le Mével

crashes hard after another rider runs into him on a wide, flat road in stage three—so hard in fact, that he thought he broke his hip. It takes a week before the Frenchman can apply full pressure to the pedals. Tyler Farrar and Murilo Fischer crash in separate incidents on stage seven. Both Farrar and Fischer drop out the next day while Le Mével soldiers on, but with his general classification chances seriously compromised.

With fellow climber Le Mével licking his wounds, Martin is the race leader. The remaining riders are workhorses: Johan Vansummeren, Andreas Klier, Sep Vanmarcke, and fellow first-time grand tour rider Andrew Talansky, an American. Aussie Heinrich Haussler rounds out the team.

Of Haussler, Vaughters says, "He needed to have a three-week stage race this year in his legs if he was going to be successful next year in the classics." In 2011 Haussler is still recovering from injuries sustained in 2010. Cycling is a chess game, with players being shifted into position months ahead of when they will be expected to make their checkmate moves. Haussler's positioning for the 2012 Spring Classics begins not next April on the Belgian cobbles, but this month on the climbs of Spain.

The stage 11 finish atop Galicia's only downhill ski area, Estación de Montaña Manzaneda, is otherworldly. A rough road cuts beneath a ski lift. On both sides of the blacktop, fields are scattered with white stones that look like the tops of skulls, while ossified sticks protruding from the muck and a scudding mist give the place the feeling of a primordial graveyard. At the finish line, there is plenty of room to sidle up to the barriers an hour before the riders are scheduled to finish. Vuelta waiters walk

up and down the barriers with trays of free tapas for spectators who arrive at the finish line on a ski lift.

When the shattered peloton finally appears, Martin finishes with the main group of climbers, including eventual race winner Juan José Cobo. At the top, he grabs tights and jacket from the soigneurs, flips a U-turn and rides back down the course, passing the rest of his teammates laboring up the 12-mile climb.

This Vuelta has been long, "really, really long," Martin says after the stage, pointing out that the peloton has had only one sprint finish in the first two weeks—a measure of the race's relentlessly hilly profile. "The profiles don't really do it justice," Martin notes of the cross-section maps in the Vuelta race bible. "There's over 55,000 meters [180,400 feet] of climbing in this race. It's just endless; every day thousands and thousands of meters of climbing." Martin is not complaining, though. "It's been exactly what I wanted, a really good test for the future as far as being a Grand Tour rider."

Vaughters will tell you again and again that he relies on empirical data when judging a rider's fitness

ABOVE Johan Vansummeren and Andreas Klier in Pontevedra. TOP RIGHT Spanish podium beauties. BOTTOM RIGHT Vuelta aficionada.

for the team and the rigors of pro level racing. But you can't measure a rider's head space by running it through a centrifuge. Martin says his psychology has held him back in the past. He admits that this Vuelta is a breakthrough. "I seem to have really grown up mentally for sure this year," he says.

Asked if his Vuelta stage win validates the work that has gone into his career, the usually incisive Irishman is at a loss for words. After a long pause, Martin says, "It's strange; I haven't really thought about it at all. I guess it's the nature of stage racing. Whether you have a good day or a bad day, you've always got the next day to change your fortune."

The following day's start is wedged into a cramped street in the interior of Ponteareas, a Galician town that has been home to three separate Vuelta winners since the race was first run in 1935. Team buses line a street so narrow it would seem to defy admitting one motorcoach, let alone 22. Yet here they all are, queued like train cars. "It's crazy," Vansummeren says, smiling wanly and waving at the babies, grandmothers, and teenagers swarming excitedly around the start area. Indeed, children are king in Spain, and while adults without press credentials are kept out of the rider sign-in area, children and their mothers are given magic dispensation to walk right in and mix with the riders.

Vansummeren says this Vuelta has been too hard and mountainous. "There were 60 people off the back in the first week," the Paris-Roubaix winner mournfully recalls. He adds that the climbs in Galicia are steep. "You break your fork when you hit them," holding his hand up like a policeman stopping traffic.

The gesture captures the essence of climbs in Galicia. Over roads trafficked by shepherds, fishermen, and smugglers for thousands of years, past heavy stone grain storage sheds and moss-covered flanks of granite, these ancient pathways do not benefit from modern road-building techniques. Unlike the roads in Colorado, built in an industrial era when machines could force mountains to bend to their will, the *caminos* in this enchanted corner of Iberia follow the topography like a ragged sea of waves. And that often means the riders face series of climbs that constantly change from wicked steep to gradual to nearly vertical again.

Stage 13 is a relatively short 98 miles. But what it lacks in distance, it makes up for in climbing. The five categorized climbs on the profile map disguise the true brutality of the stage, which takes the riders out of hilly Galicia into the savagery of the Cantabrian Mountains. Known as the Cordillera Cantábrica, this 180-mile long mountain range lies like a policeman's spike strip between Spain's high plains and its Atlantic coast.

Near the base of the day's second climb, the 3,330-foot Alto de O Lago, locals in wool sweaters and tracksuits cluster on a cliff overlook. Below, a clutch of red-roofed houses curl up against green valley walls. A break goes through. No Garmin-Cervélo riders are in it, and the break stays away for the duration. When the field labors through the hairpins of the Alto de O Lago, Martin sits comfort-

ably in the lead group, where he stays for the rest of the day. The other team riders follow toward the rear of the peloton. The days of the Garmin-Cervélo boys animating every break and forcing the pace are suspended at the Vuelta. This is just surviving.

After the team suffers through 13 days of stage racing, the team hotel, a windswept glass and marble place 25 miles from Portugal and within shouting distance of two neon-signed motorway brothels, has the vibe of a field hospital. In one room, soigneur Sandra Ni Hodnae kneads the lactic acid out of Dan Martin's muscles. While she

OPPOSITE The green hills of Galicia. TOP RIGHT Dan Martin scales the Alto de O Lago. RIGHT In the laughing group, Johan Vansummeren and Heinrich Haussler ride through stage 14's Cantabrian ravines.

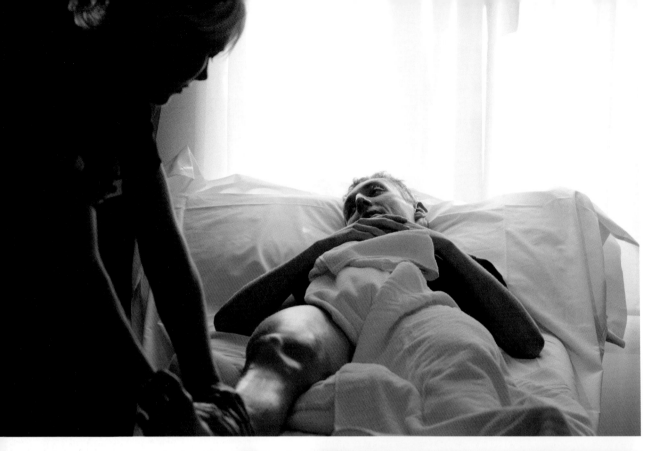

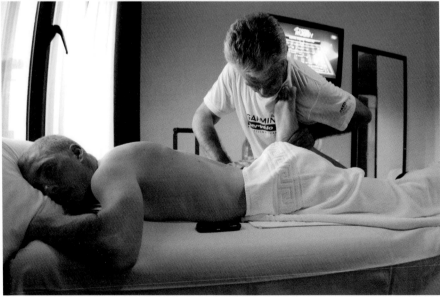

works, director Bingen Fernandez talks quietly with the Irishman. "How do you feel?" Looking as weary as he sounds, Martin tells his director he's tapped out. "It was fucking crazy today. Just full gas."

Later that night, Martin has an appointment with team chiropractor Kevin Reichlin. Wearing gray sweatpants and a black Garmin-Cervélo T-shirt, Martin sits on a massage table. His back has been bothering him since he won the 6,463-foot-high mountain stage five days ago. Reichlin probes, "How did you feel today?"

The Irishman says he feels the effect of not drinking or eating for the final 12 miles today. "Crazy downhills and gravel," he says, shaking his head. "The roads are so narrow that the team cars can't get up to us to give us bottles."

After confirming that Martin has been making up for the lack of food and hydration, Reichlin directs him to lie on his side. The chiropractor leans into Martin, pushing down on his back and hip like an auto body repairman flexing a door panel. Martin groans. Reichlin repeats. Then he pushes the Irishman's legs, at once testing and rehabilitating. "Does that hurt?"

"That's better than yesterday," Martin replies.

After 30 minutes of chiropractic work that leave Martin looking more buggered than when he came through the door, Reichlin picks up a device that emits slices of red light. "Class-three cold laser," he explains. According to Reichlin, the lasers affect ATP production and help with recovery and healing at the cellular level. Martin lies on his back and closes his eyes. Holding the device between his index and middle finger, Reichlin runs the red laser beams across Martin's hip and stomach. The twin lines drag back and forth like glowing red spatula blades. The process has a soothingly ritualistic air.

"Relax," Reichlin tells Martin. He repeats the process then says, "One more time on your back." Reichlin is not hurried, but he is firm. He also prefaces each adjustment to Martin's body with an explanation: "This is what we are going to do next, OK?" He waits for a response before proceeding.

As Reichlin packs up his lasers and readies them for the next rider, Martin squirts a topical cream on his fingers and rubs it into his lower back. "Shit, that's burning like hell. Wow!" he exclaims. Reichlin smiles. The balm contains menthol and chili pepper extract. "That's the thing about grand tours," Reichlin comments. "They just start beating guys up."

Kevin Reichlin rehabilitates Dan Martin with chiropractic and cold laser treatments.

THE NEXT DAY'S 14TH STAGE TAKES THE riders from the lovely stone-walled Roman town of Astorga to a mountaintop finish at Lagos de Somiedo, high in the Cantabrian Mountains. At the start, which is sunny but with a whisper of September 3rd's autumnal chill in the air, Vansummeren rides down a crowd-lined chute toward the sign-in stage, which is set below Astorga's ornate cathedral. The announcer spots the Belgian getting off his bike and winds up the crowd with a 100-mph speech about the arrival of the 2011 Paris-Roubaix winner. Vansummeren walks slowly across the stage, signs in, and waves shyly.

As the peloton gathers for the start in Astorga's restaurant-lined plaza, Le Mével jokes with Italian sprinting star Alessandro Petacchi and 2008 Tour de France champion Carlos Sastre. Shortly after

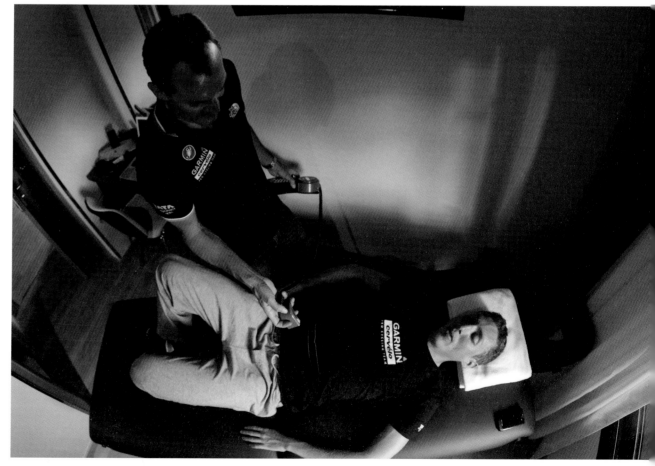

ABOVE Before a fateful stage 14, Sep Vanmarcke signs in with eventual Vuelta winner Juan Jose Cobo. RIGHT Christophe Le Mével in Astorga. OPPOSITE After crashing into a tree, Sep Vanmarcke emerges from a ravine.

riding onto the high, dry plains of Leon that surround the town, Vanmarcke gets in a break. His lead stretches to nearly eight minutes. Then, descending the first major climb of the day, the category two Puerto de La Ventana, Vanmarcke disappears off the edge of a road into a forest. No one sees him go over. Nor does anyone see BMC rider Kaarsten Kroon slip over the guardrail.

"Suddenly there was a corner to the left," Vanmarcke recounts after the stage. "You couldn't see that it was going to be so short." When Kroon wipes out, Vanmarcke runs into him. "I went straight over the barrier," he says, sighing. "I flew 40 meters. A tree stopped me, and I was like 5 meters away from a river."

"What were you thinking after you hit the tree?" I ask.

"That I'm lucky? Not many people survive a crash of 40 meters. When I came down, I heard someone else crashing also, and that was Karsten Kroon. Then they start looking for him, and I started screaming because no one could see me. I was too far down."

Race radio does not know about the crash, so the team cars following both the break and the peloton pass Vanmarcke, leaving him stranded in the ravine. When a team support car finally makes it back up to the crash scene, Sep has pulled himself out of the ravine by tree branches. On his way he collects his bike, which is stuck in the woods 10 meters below

the road. He crawls over the guardrail, gets back on, and starts riding.

But the 23-year-old from Kortrijk, Belgium, is shaken. So much so that he cannot follow wheels on the downhills. "I was even worse than a tourist. I had a lot of pain, and mentally I was totally broken," he recalls later. Vaughters calls Vanmarcke "über-enthusiastic, young, strong. He's probably the next great classics rider." That strength, as much mental as physical, surfaces when Vanmarcke chases and eventually rejoins the gruppetto, the last group of nonclimbers on the road. Vanmarcke weeps as he rides. "At that moment you just realize what you survived," he says. "I was totally mentally broken. I started crying for two hours. I couldn't stop. I had no power. I was shocked."

During those hours going over two more categorized climbs, Andreas Klier and 2008 Ronde van Vlaanderen winner and fellow Belgian Stijn Devolder ride alongside. Vanmarcke says having Klier at this side during the most trying hours of his career was like having family with him.

Vanmarcke looks at his hands resting in his lap. He is touched. "In the gruppetto those two guys stayed with me and helped me. It was really nice of them." And on the topic of family, after Wouter Weylandt's death at the Giro, Vanmarcke is grateful his parents were not watching on TV when he crashed. To hear that he disappeared over the guardrail, "then after 10 minutes, nothing," is something he would not want them to suffer.

Christophe Le Mével, here on the 104-mile stage 14 to Lagos de Somiedo, at first thought he had broken his hip in a crash on stage 3.

STAGE 15, 88 MILES LONG, FINISHES ATOP one of the world's most devastating climbs, the 8-mile path to the 5,167-foot height of Asturias's Alto de L'Angliru. Approaching the turnoff to the climb, stone houses cling like spiders to valleys slashed into the Cantabrian Mountains. A dog rests with his head on his paws, eyes trained on a flock of sheep grazing on a 45-degree-angle field beneath him. The area feels as much like Tibet as Spain. It's not the place for a cyclist to recover from a 40-meter fall into a ravine.

Twenty-eight miles after the start in Avilés, an estuary town on the Cantabrian Sea, the field ramps up for an intermediate sprint, and a rider wipes out in front of Vansummeren. The Paris-Roubaix winner plows into him and crashes on top of a cylindrical traffic pylon. Though the green traffic-control device is designed to forgive when a 3,000-pound automobile hits it, it becomes a hard, sharp, flesh-sampling tool when it meets Vansummeren's meager 167 pounds.

Team physician Serge Niamke is an emergency room doctor who has seen plenty of gore, but he winces when he arrives at the crash site. Vansummeren, his front soaked with blood, is bent over with pain and clutching himself. Niamke takes one look and urges, "Johan, let's get into the ambulance." Vansummeren's body is sliced, and his testicles are smashed. "When I arrived, the race doctor already had his hands down Johan's shorts," Niamke recalls, "to see if he was badly hurt." The Vuelta doctor also implores Vansummeren to get into the ambulance.

ABOVE Angliru vista. LEFT Spanish horses climb the Angliru.

Dan Martin grinds up a 23 percent grade on the Angliru.

"Where is my bike? Where is my bike?" Vansummeren responds. Deaf to the doctors' entreaties, he insists, "No, no, no. Give me my bike!" The Belgian gets on his Cervélo and chases back to the field, but not without first taking a bag of ice and shoving it down his bib shorts. "He just got on his bike and went," mechanic Joan Linares recalls, his voice lowered in awe. "The ice froze his balls, put them to sleep."

Hours later, Vansummeren and the rest of the battered team reach the bottom of the Angliru. The climb ascends a road no wider than a bike path. First raced in the Vuelta in 1999, in its steepest sections the grade strikes chain-breaking ratios of 23.5 percent. While the steepness is amazing, it's even more astonishing to think that someone had the audacity to pave this cliff-side goat track.

At 5,100 feet, one kilometer from the finish, gray clouds rush over the spongy alpine tundra. A brief hole in the clouds reveals a patchwork of green pastures below. Asturias is utterly breathtaking. Also visible is a ridge—the only place where it's possible to park on the climb—sprinkled with a confetti of fans' camping tents. The aficionados gathered at the 1-kilometer kite are dedicated. They all either rode bikes or made a four-hour hike from the bottom.

Eventual Vuelta winner Cobo rides past to a solo stage victory; 1:41 later, Martin appears below on the road that spills down the stepped cliff face like a casually dropped rope. Pushing a 34 x 28 gear, his face is twisted with pain. Martin goes on to place 11th that day. After the stage, Martin, who comes alive when the road lurches up, laughs and admits that the "24 percent bit was a bit too steep!" He says he could have used a 30-tooth cog on the back to give him "a bit more fluidity."

Le Mével labors through three minutes later, and then the survivors' march begins. Vanmarcke rides over a field of white graffiti that Basque fans painted across the road. A fan in a red and white cycling kit and a mountain bike helmet runs alongside, pushing him up the hill. The process repeats again and again with other riders, some of them imploring the fans for "a push, a push."

In exchange for the assist, riders hand off water bottles to the fans. Some have already bartered away their bottles. Their gloveless hands show that anything that can be disconnected has been exchanged for an upward shove against the cruel climb.

Vanmarcke digs into his back pocket, extracts his last packet of Clif Shot Bloks and hands it to the man in red and white. "I gave everything," Vanmarcke later says. He is speaking both literally and figuratively. "It hurted so much, my back," he recalls in careful, but somewhat halting English. "I still have no power. Every help I could get I was thankful." Handing fans his food "was the only thing I could do. To show my thanks I was giving my things away."

As Vansummeren arrives, the clouds suddenly drop onto the road, and he rides through fog. Weak sunlight inscribes a rim of light around his pain-wracked visage. Though fans push him, he does not seem to notice. He is mentally in another place. Between the crash and this horrific climb—a kilometer shorter than l'Alpe d'Huez, but twice as steep—Vansummeren looks more like a soldier who stepped out of Spain's horrifying Civil War than an elite athlete.

At the hotel that night, Niamke examines Vansummeren; the crash into the pylon earlier in the day also tore open his elbow. "I give him stitches in two places," the French doctor explains as he shares a glass of wine with the beer-drinking mechanics at the hotel bar. "Four to close one cut, three to close another. So tough, man, so tough."

After dinner, Vansummeren offers an Angliru stage précis: "It wasn't too nice." He dodders past the curious gaze of the brunette hotel receptionist, white bandages covering the sutures in his elbow. Waiting for the elevator to take him to his room, to rest at last, he says, "It's a shit race. But it's part of the job, huh?"

I sit down with Andrew Talansky to find out how he's managing his job as a grand tour water

TOP Sep Vanmarcke gives Clif Shot Bloks in thanks for a push up the Angliru. ABOVE Andrew Talansky gets an assist from a willing Basque supporter.

TOP LEFT Johan Vansummeren hours after a traumatic run-in with road furniture. TOP RIGHT Andreas Klier shows the strain of a brutal Vuelta. OPPOSITE The race enters the high plains of Castile-Leon.

carrier. Along with Vanmarcke, this is the 23-year-old American's first grand tour, and it's a leap, considering that not long ago he was riding for little more than expenses with a minor team on the U.S. domestic circuit. Talansky is getting a massage from Vincente Pana, a craggy Spaniard whose hands are muscled by the 31 years he has spent as a Vuelta soigneur.

While Pana works Talansky's legs like a potter molding clay, the neo pro marvels that a year ago he was doing Tour de l'Avenir. That French stage race for riders under 23 is a coming-out event for many top pros. "That was a supposedly hard race," Talansky says of the eight-day event. But now, with 13 stages of the Vuelta in his legs, it seems like "a piece of cake—a tricycle race compared to this thing."

Now that he has grand tour experience, Talansky is astonished where life has taken him. "It's just all in perspective. Two years ago I remember I was getting dropped at the Tour of Utah, finishing toward

the back. It's interesting how things work out, and it's fun sometimes to look back."

Talansky can be at once as nervous and reposeful as a cat. At the stage 14 start in Astorga, as the race announcer makes his final staging call, Talansky gets off his bike and pushes his thumb down on his rear tire, checking its pressure. The mechanics have already topped off all the riders' tubulars, but Talansky asks Alex Banyay to check the wheel again, just in case. What is it that separated Talansky from the hundreds of other talented young riders trying to make it on the North American circuit? Talansky ponders the question carefully. "You really have to want it. There are times when others are going to question what you are doing. But if you have enough belief in yourself and you have the talent to do it, then you can make it."

Talansky started riding as a kid in Florida, where he was a runner in high school. "I grew up in a bathing suit and sandals," he says, noting that

The team in survival mode.

surfing was his first sport. "It's very peaceful, you know. Kind of like why I like being around people in cycling who really ride because they love the bike. Nobody is out there surfing for money or thinks like that. Everybody just wants to enjoy it."

As a young man who left college early to gamble on a career in pro cycling, the professional turmoil that roils his sport weighs on him. And he's not afraid to share his feelings about both how he thinks his profession needs to change and Vaughters's efforts to make that revolution happen. Talansky believes many of the people leading cycling governance today have short-term vision. "They don't care what happens when they leave, whether it's a rider or a director. They care about getting as much as they can for themselves."

From Talansky's point of view, "Jonathan, he really has never seemed to care too much about what he himself gets. He'd be fine without cycling, but he loves it, so he invests his time and energy and effort into this team and trying to represent the needs and wants of the riders." For Talansky, the fact that Vaughters has interests beyond cycling gives him greater moral authority as a leader, "because he would be just fine without cycling."

In contrast, Talansky says, look at other directors in the sport, and their career options today remain what they were when they started as neo pros: "Man, they have no choice. The other option when they were younger was some manual labor job. So they shut up and take their paycheck and say, 'You should be thankful for what you have.'" Talansky is careful to point out that he is grateful for his dream life, but—and this is perhaps where his restless American spirit comes through—for him thankfulness does not equate to acquiescence. "It's not about being ungrateful." Talansky points out that cyclists deliver fan entertainment and sponsor brand exposure. Theirs is a commercial arrangement. "As long as we are paid to go ride our bikes, there is no reason why we shouldn't make sure that we are treated fairly and paid accordingly."

The race radio controversy bubbling away throughout the season is a proxy for a larger struggle over power and rights in the sport. One way the UCI has attempted to corral power is to infantilize riders by pointing out that their own house is not in order with regards to doping. This broad-brushing of the entire peloton deeply offends Talansky. A March 2011 open letter from UCI president Pat McQuaid to the professional riders intimates that

if the riders are not grown-up enough to clean up their doping act, they haven't earned the right to weigh in on radios and how the sport should be governed. "Riders, too, often tend to forget their role and their responsibilities: There are bigger problems in our sport which need your attention," the letter says.

"When you have the head of the sport making statements that not all the riders are clean, it's a really unfortunate thing," Talansky fumes. "It's a little bit sad, and it really makes you question what their intentions are." Even as Pana works his legs into a state of buttery suppleness, Talansky's brow knits and his voice rises. The UCI's suggestion that Talansky is not doing all he can to ride clean offends

"It's been exactly what I wanted," said Dan Martin of his Vuelta, "a really good test for the future."

After traumatic crashes during week two, Sep Vanmarcke (left) and Johan Vansummeren breakfast during Vuelta week three.

in the sport of cycling and doesn't deserve to write about it."

Talansky explains that there are other clean teams out there, and he feels it's unjust of someone like Kimmage to only focus on Garmin-Cervélo while tarring the rest of the peloton. "I'm really sad for him," he confides. "It is puzzling to me why these people are still around the sport. . . . I get a little angry about that."

ON SEPTEMBER 6, THE MORNING OF STAGE 16, Andreas Klier sits alone at the dining room at the team's hotel in Palencia, a town of about 80,000, set on the high plains of Castile-Leon's Meseta Central. "Up at six to piss," he says with Teutonic directness. The doping vampires knocked at his door that morning for a sample. They also collect from Heinrich Haussler, but not the rest of the team.

With the sun just coming over the edge of the Spanish plains outside, Klier sits at the table with director Bingen Fernandez. As they discuss the logistics of getting Klier's bikes to Copenhagen for the world championships in a few weeks, team chef Sean Fowler walks in with a big metal pot of smoothies. Behind the hotel in his cooking van, Fowler uncovers a leg of Spanish Serrano ham that is carved down to the bone. "We go through one about every two weeks," he observes before rushing up to the dining room with a platter of fluffy pancakes.

The rest of the team filters in. Talansky pours himself a bowl of granola. When he learns that the manufacturer, a small U.S. company called Bakery

him. "People can speculate, people can say what they want. But I can tell you that guys like Tejay van Garteren, guys like Taylor Phinney, people like myself, everybody on my team . . . it's just not accepted now."

Talansky is visibly saddened when he talks about fans and journalists who don't believe any riders are clean. Yet, upon hearing that doping denouncer Paul Kimmage finds Vaughters's team a beacon of hope, a shadow crosses Talansky's face again. "I think it's great" that Garmin-Cervélo gives Kimmage hope, he says. Then he adds, darkly, "I also think that somebody like him has no place on Main, is sponsoring the team, he is delighted. "Really? This stuff is the best!" Martin finds out that both Klier and Haussler had to pee for the drug testers and throws them a poke. "You guys are going too fast in the gruppetto!" Haussler is his usual droll self, making gangster signs with his hands and mugging for the camera.

Vansummeren, Klier, and Vanmarcke don't smile. They are lean cuts of aching discomfort. Thwacked, hammered, and wrung by the taxing Vuelta course and run-ins with trees and road fixtures, the riders show the rough side of pro cycling. Every rider at the table has reached the acme of sport, they are living the dream. Yet their breakfast table lassitude— another hotel ballroom at sunrise, another bowl of oatmeal—suggests the life of a draft horse rather than an international sporting star. While the Tour de France saw the team riding a three-week rush of success, the Vuelta shows most of the team crashed out and flogging themselves at the back of the pack.

After breakfast, the team mounts up and rides from the first-century Roman settlement of Villa Romana la Olmeda—B.C.-era tile mosaics and building walls plopped, literally, in the middle of vast, empty plains—to Haro in the Rioja wine region. Haussler is right there at the tip of the peloton in the final sprint, but is foiled when a rider in front of him follows a motorcycle the wrong way on a roundabout 300 meters from the finish. Crossing the finish line, his eyes cast about menacingly, looking for the perpetrator of his downfall. The race's arrival five days later in Madrid sees Martin move into 13th place overall, the team's top-ranked rider at the Vuelta. But by then, the cycling world's attention is turning back to the New World.

In Spain, kids are king. Heinrich Haussler signs autographs for happy fans—and their mothers.

quarter filled with boutique hotels, romantic bistros, and granite lanes in a city that was founded in 1608, 600 years after that other Norwegian, Leif Ericson, established the first European settlement in North America in Newfoundland. Sunday features a 128-mile race in Montréal, Canada's second-biggest city, some 150 miles to the southwest of Québec City.

But the racing actually gets started on Thursday, with a sprint competition in Québec City. Each team enters a single rider in the event. Four riders at a time start a 1-kilometer sprint—500 meters down Rue Saint Louis, under an arched gateway in the old city's massive stone fortification walls, then 500 meters back up. The top two placers move on to the next round until only four riders are left for the final heat. The Challenge Sprint is a spectator-friendly setup, with big-screen TVs showing the entire 1-kilometer race. Later heats delight the crowds when riders slow to a near stop as they position themselves for the final 200-meter sprint.

Stetina is Garmin's entry. A mountain climber, he does not typically spend much time doing sprints or track stands. Before his heat, he sits bemusedly in a tent behind the starting ramp. He doesn't make it to the final round. After his heat, I ask if he regrets missing the Vuelta, which wraps up in two days in Madrid. "No way," he responds without hesitation. "That's a dying race."

Serge Arsenault, a 63-year-old Canadian with three decades of television broadcasting experience, is both the brainchild and the bank behind the sprint and the Québec and Montréal events, which are in their second year. As someone who built a business in television broadcasting, Arsenault knows what it's like to be on the buying side of sports entertainment. He explains that broadcasters want a professionally produced, well-packaged product. The new sprint event is designed to meet that need. Ninety minutes from first rider to last, the event builds suspense and finishes with an explosive finale, and it is easy to understand. It is a tightly crafted television product that makes bike racing appealing to broadcasters around the world.

"We have to respect what was done and the classical cycling disciplines," Arsenault explains, referring to the two road races that follow the Challenge Sprint. However, he says the sport can better grow by capitalizing on what he sees as a massive base of support among the bike-buying public. "We have to mix what we have right now with one or two new concepts," he explains. "That way when you approach the TV guys, you can say, 'OK, we have a concept that is nearly made for TV.'" And by that, he means for the public, for sponsors, and for broadcasters. This is the first year Arsenault has done the Challenge Sprint. Sixty-five broadcasters signed up to televise it, and a total of 106 broadcasters around the world will show the road races. Arsenault says he is not yet breaking even on the $4.5 million he invested in the race weekend, but expects to next year.

At the sprint turnaround point, Glenn and Cathy Goodman are two Canadian spectators who agree that North America is the place to be for September racing. Glenn, who looks to be about 50, came to the inaugural version of this race last year and says he "was surprised by how many fans there were here." Cycling appeals to him because when he rides he likes "the freedom on the road—the ability to kind of dump the brain."

Goodman says he has followed racing since the Merckx era in the 1970s. Watching the racing in Québec is "a spectacle unto itself. It's like Formula One car racing in terms of its intensity and just the skill level." He is tuned in to the cultural changes in the sport. "I think there is a more level playing field." Yet he never minded doping scandals. "Riding is riding, racing is racing, and the spectacle is everything."

The next day it is sunny and 70 degrees at the Grand Prix Cycliste de Quebéc start. At the sign-in stage, the announcer introduces Belgian Philippe Gilbert to a volume of applause that shows these fans know their pro cycling. Canadian schoolchildren line up in front of the stage and hold on to the riders' Cervélos, while they sign in and pose for photos. The announcer welcomes Hesjedal, and a bigger wave of cheering than Gilbert elicited washes through the crowd. Hesjedal bows slightly to the adoring countrymen who, in a Canadian cycling magazine poll, named him cyclist of the decade.

Wilson, Zabriskie, Vande Velde, and HTC rider Danny Pate sit for 20 minutes drinking coffee in the departure village behind the sign-in stage, then return to the start line, and the race gets going. The scene feels European in this French-speaking city. Fans sit at bars and cafés lining the course and hang off walls, lampposts, and a bridge on a steep, curving climb that passes under battlements that once protected the French settlement from British and American invaders. With about 40 miles

OPPOSITE TOP Ryder Hesjedal gives a EuroSport interview at the Château Frontenac. OPPOSITE BOTTOM Mechanic's all-access pass. RIGHT Peter Stetina awaits his turn in the Québec Sprint Challenge.

remaining, the Garmin-Cervélo riders make their way to the front of the race on the challenging 8-mile circuit. Passing under the stone arches that mark seventeenth-century Québec City, Stetina gasses it. The field strings out behind him, but he does not escape. A few laps later, the entire team masses at the front in an effort to bring back a three-man break.

Then Vande Velde attacks the field; it looks like textbook teamwork, as the other teams are forced to chase or let the dangerous Garmin-Cérvelo rider get away. They bring him back, and then, passing the stout stone Martello cannon towers on the Plains of Abraham, site of a fierce battle in the French and Indian War 252 years ago almost to this day, Hesjedal puts his head down and presses on the pedals to bring back the break. Backlit by the dropping Indian summer sun, Hesjedal, with Olympic Gold medalist Samuel Sanchez on his wheel, cuts a desperate but ultimately defeated figure at the head of the field. He's caught, and Philippe Gilbert goes on to add another win to his season.

The next morning the team boards a train that takes them from Québec to Montréal. Meanwhile, mechanics Geoff Brown and Eric Fostvedt drive the mechanic trailer and bikes to the city of 2 million. There they unfold the doors of the trailer in a downtown canyon formed by the race hotel on one side and an office tower on the other.

That afternoon, the riders head out and do a few laps on the 7.5-mile course loop that starts in central Montréal and passes through the city's wooded 494-acre Mount Royal Park, site of the 1976 Olympic road race. A stream of fans strolls past the trailer. A young girl in a Garmin-Cérvelo

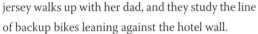

jersey walks up with her dad, and they study the line of backup bikes leaning against the hotel wall.

Clairese Wilson is nine. Her dad, James, says they have a special connection with this squad because the team reaches out to them through the *Beyond the Peloton* Internet films. Speaking with startling rhetorical precision, Clairese tells me she likes Heinrich Haussler because "I read that he is one of the best." She rides a road bike "because it's an endurance sport; you can go for long rides." Clairese's mom, Stephanie, hangs back a few feet. She has one eye on her daughter and the other on a

homeless guy down the block shouting at the sky in French. Stephanie admits that the family does not watch much TV, but when they do it tends to be bike racing. "As a family, we like people who achieve their best. We look for people who work hard. We appreciate that."

A couple hours after they leave, the team reappears, swooping out of the early fall sun into the shadows of the concrete canyon. Four or five recreational riders, teenagers, follow them like pilot fish. Zabriskie doesn't stop, but rides up a plywood ramp and is swallowed into the mouth of the trailer. The

OPPOSITE TOP Dave Zabriskie, Ryder Hesjedal, Michel Kreder, and Peter Stetina (left to right) on the Québec City sign-in stage. OPPOSITE BOTTOM Zabriskie in old Québec City. ABOVE LEFT The peloton streams past the Saint Laurence River. ABOVE RIGHT Climbing to the citadel walls.

kids ask the riders for their bottles, and one young man is astonished when Vande Velde says, "Sure, go for it. My bike is there." The boy approaches Vande Velde's Cervélo and gingerly pulls the bottle out of the cage.

Danielson asks Geoff Brown to adjust his rear derailleur. A teenager approaches with a tattered leather book and collects a signature from him. "Where is Tom Peterson?" Brown asks. "He's doing another lap," Wilson responds. Twenty minutes later, Peterson rolls in with the red-kitted Cofidis team. He hands the bike to Brown and says, "The rear derailleur is making some noise." Brown puts it on the stand and starts an examination.

Later, Fostvedt sits in the doorway of the trailer and plays a harmonica. Laughing, he takes his baseball cap off and places it upside down on the sidewalk in front of him. Cervélo's Tom Fowler and company cofounder Phil White approach from down the street and go inside the hotel. Minutes later, Vaughters approaches from the direction of the shouting homeless guy. Dressed in a vest and tie and clutching a crumpled street map, he cuts the figure of a disoriented British tourist fresh off a flight from Heathrow. "Have you guys seen Matt Johnson or Tom Fowler and Gerard?" Vaughters asks, referring to the team president and the Cervélo head honchos. "We have a meeting." Brown points toward the hotel entrance.

SEPTEMBER 11 DAWNS WITH THE SAME achingly blue sky that the Northeast saw on a tragic day a decade ago. Fans in the VIP area next to the

sign-in stage sip champagne and coffee. When Hesjedal steps onto the stage, the announcer ramps up the volume on his first name like a roller coaster car, a drawn out *Ryyyyyderrr* followed by a rushing *Hesjedal!* Before the stage start, race organizer Arsenault takes the microphone and asks for a

OPPOSITE Matt Wilson with one lap to go in Montréal. LEFT A 125-mile race at season's end pulls sweat from Tom Danielson. BELOW From 11th, Ryder Hesjedal watches Rui Costa (out of photo) win in Montréal.

moment of silence. The peloton bows all heads and a hush descends upon the fans pressed against the fence. Then the race is on.

Garmin-Cervélo makes an immediate appearance in the 17-lap race, when Stetina and Zabriskie get to the front and force the pace on lap two. Halfway through the race, a stream of fans walks past the feed zone tent. While Fostvedt naps, soigneur Alyssa Morahan looks up from Facebook on her mobile phone to tell a group of souvenir-hungry teenage girls, "Sorry, we only have bottles for the riders." Walking away, one of the girls looks back at the rainbow striped bottles and longingly says, "Oh, the Garmin bottles are soooo nice."

LEFT Québec feels like Europe, but the racing is distinctively New World. ABOVE Dave Zabriskie and Tom Peterson in Québec. OPPOSITE (Right to left) Ryder Hesjedal, Tom Danielson, Levi Leipheimer, Christian Vande Velde, George Hincapie, and Philippe Gilbert at the Montréal start.

LEFT (3) Ryder Hesjedal with Gavin King and the press after Montréal. RIGHT Peter Stetina under Québec walls.

With about 20 miles remaining, Danielson clips off the front in a large breakaway, which is eventually partially absorbed by the field. Vande Velde lays down a savage attack on Mount Royal, a hill that in addition to the 1976 Olympics figured in the world championships road course where Eddy Merckx took the gold in 1974—the same season he also won the Tour de France and the Giro d'Italia. Vande Velde's attack allows Hesjedal to mark race favorites Gilbert, Levi Leipheimer, and Dutchman Robert Gesink, but in the meantime three other opportunists get away without Vande Velde or Hesjedal. On the final lap, Hesjedal doesn't have enough left to bring back race winner Rui Costa.

Hesjedal stops on the other side of the finish line. "Eleventh," he says with disgust. "Fuck! That's the *worst* place." Last year Hesjedal placed third here and fourth in Québec. The outburst is striking; Hesjedal is normally a cool pool of calm, but now, he seems on the verge of tears. Soigneur Gavin King hands Hesjedal a bottle of water then wipes his sweat-glistening face with a towel mitt. While a massive Sunday drum circle smokes and throbs in the park behind him, Hesjedal begins responding to questions from reporters. "The team were all great. Tom and Christian were right there at the end. Just not enough horsepower from behind."

TOP LEFT Ryder Hesjedal on Québec's Plains of Abraham. TOP RIGHT Hesjedal poses with fans. MIDDLE RIGHT Mapleleaf power. ABOVE Grand Prix Québec and Montréal organizer Serge Arsenault.

ABOVE North American cycling passion. OPPOSITE
Peter Stetina, delighted to be racing in North America,
not Spain.

Hesjedal makes a trip to the podium to collect his award as best-finishing Canadian. That earns him a trip to the press conference. Usually Marya Pongrace would accompany him to the conference and watch nervously from the sidelines. But the PR director is not here, so soigneur Alyssa Morahan escorts him to an enclosed white tent behind the finish line. His season is over with this race, Hesjedal tells the journalists. The world

championship course in two weeks in Copenhagen is too flat; it's not worth going back to Europe for a race that will end in a bunch sprint. His goals for next year? "Get the year going early" by racing January's Tour Down Under in Australia, then focus on the Ardennes Classics and the Tour of the Basque Country.

Hesjedal walks out of the press conference into a pack of kids waiting outside in the matching cycling club kits. Though he raced nearly five and a half hours today, he stops. One boy asks Hesjedal to sign his shirt, another, a magazine with the Garmin-Cervélo rider on the cover. The kids quickly pick up on Hesjedal's amenability. His patience suggests a kinship, a propinquity in common cycling values that melts the ceremonious space the kids at first keep between themselves and a man who is, in their eyes, a god. They draw closer to him and one another until finally Hesjedal is piled right in there posing for a group portrait. A mom can hardly contain herself as she snaps the photo. Obviously touched, she nervously blurts out, "We are a team, part of the same club."

Hesjedal then rides slowly toward the high rises of downtown Montréal. "I remember being a kid," Hesjedal says of the autograph seekers. "Looking up to all the guys in the magazines." Those images gave him the impression that cycling was a life option. "That's what I wanted to do."

Hesjedal explains that while he knows he may affect those youngsters in the same way photos of cycling heroes changed him, the eager boys and girls also motivate him. The children give him the lift of a nation. "It helps me because I know that I'm inspiring kids. It's gratifying, and it's just neat to be in that role."

Gratitude and its variations populate Hesjedal's thoughts. The idea of thankfulness for those around him comes up repeatedly in our conversations here and elsewhere throughout the season. From beneath his unruffled mien, Hesjedal seems to peer out with astonishment at the opportunities life offers him, from the fiancée he adores to this WorldTour race in his native land. Arsenault does

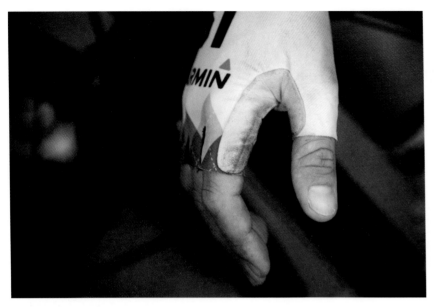

ABOVE Hesjdal's hand. RIGHT Peter Stetina, tapped out by five and a half hours of September racing. OPPOSITE Bird's-eye peloton view above Montréal.

not yet break even on these races. And Hesjedal is thankful for the sacrifice. "It's a huge gift," Hesjedal says of Arsenault's events.

Looking back over the year, Hesjedal professes that the Tour of the Basque Country was a highlight. The craggy six-day race is known as the most difficult stage race next to the Tour de France. Hesjedal nods his head with satisfaction as he ponders his ninth place overall. "I was really on track, I was stronger than I was last spring, but it didn't correlate to results in the Ardennes."

Ryder is very strong, Vaughters says when explaining why he brought him onto the team from U.S. domestic squad Health Net in 2008. "And he's very focused in his training." According to Vaughters, that concentration paid off in July at the Tour de France team time trial, a discipline that has traditionally been a weakness for the Canadian. "He really put it together for that day."

Hesjedal is also thankful that, while he crashed twice at the Tour, he did not crash out like Zabriskie, or get car-launched into a barbed wire fence like Dutchman Johnny Hoogerland and Spaniard Juan Antonio Flecha. "At the end of the day, it was positive," Hesjedal says of his stage-one crash only 5 miles from the finish line that saw him go over his bars, lose two minutes, and plummet to 96th place overall. Of that spill and his participation in a mass pileup on stage seven, he reflects, "I learned more from that experience than if everything went perfectly. I'm still happy with the outcome, what I was able to do in the last week."

And then there are the overall team successes at the team time trial and stage 16 to Gap where Hesjedal was instrumental in luring Edvald Boasson Hagen out from a three-man breakaway and setting up Hushovd for the win. Slowing his bike to a stop, he looks at me and says, "To be a part

of that, I mean that was just a huge success, and it's the biggest race of the year."

As for his result today, Hesjedal says his disappointment with 11th stems more from his results last year. Along with his 2010 third and fourth, he took the most combative prize in both Québec and Montréal. "Once you have those experiences, it's hard to settle for anything else. The bar is really high for me here." He brushes aside a suggestion that he's feeling the weight of the nation. "Nah—I have that pressure because I know I have that opportunity."

Some riders, like Dan Martin, seem to want to win almost entirely because of intrinsic drive. The will to be over the line first is fueled by genetically engineered internal fires. "A born winner," as Vaughters put it. In Hesjedal's case, internal drive is of course there—"Ryder can be stubborn"—but his will to seek victory seems to derive as much from extrinsic climate as internal composition. The world plopped Hesjedal into a juncture of circumstances it gives to only a tiny slice of humankind. Hesjedal takes that gift seriously, and his sense of obligation to fulfill "that opportunity" seems equal to his inner compulsion to succeed.

That said, Vaughters feels Hesjedal could profit by taking on a bit more of Martin's hell-for-leather approach to racing. To move up a spot from his 2010 second place at Amstel Gold or to win Liège-Bastogne-Liège, the team director says, "it's gonna take risk-taking on his part." Vaughters explains that Hesjedal "likes to sit at the back of the field and wait for a certain moment with 28K to go or whatever it is, when he is in the exact same spot where he did it the year before." To win a classic, Hesjedal needs to be less predictable: "Get in a breakaway that jumps the gun—that is a little bit ahead of the curve." But according to Vaughters, to do that, to get away early with a group of underestimated riders and then continue on to a win, will require Hesjedal to come to terms with his aversion to risk.

When he has a disappointing finish like today's, who or what does Hesjedal turn to for resuscitation? "We are getting married in December," he responds. He first met his fiancée, Ashley Hofer, two years ago in Boulder, Colorado, then they met again in Girona. "She's inspiration for me. She gives me the motivation." The couple will wed in Saint Louis, Missouri, her hometown. "This is just bike racing," Hesjedal adds, contextualizing the day and year. Creating a future with Hofer "is a huge part of my life. To have someone that's willing to commit to me and go into life with that, that's huge."

OPPOSITE Michel Kreder in Parc du Mont-Royal. BELOW Canadian names on the course at the University of Montréal.

THE BUSINESS
OF PRO CYCLING

9

In October, Slipstream announces a coming-out party for 2012. They will hold a team presentation in November at the Boulder Theater in their hometown.

Vaughters starts working on a separate presentation that he will make to the team. "How do you seem like you are one of the biggest teams in the world when on a budget standpoint you really aren't?" Vaughters muses on the mid-October afternoon he sits down to outline his talk. He wants to unveil for his 2012 squad—a mix of 11 new and 19 returning riders—an understanding of the economics of their sport and team. Specifically, he wants to present the financial calculus behind how, through teamwork, they will deliver results on par with their big-money competitors, but with half the budget.

One of his presentation slides is a bar chart showing Slipstream's annual budget compared to other WorldTour teams. Slipstream is on the low-budget side of the graph, a modest column less than half the height of the Rabobank and BMC towers, which sit somewhere between 25 and 30 million euros ($32–39 million).

Another bar chart shows the team's "sporting value" according to the ranking system the UCI employs when granting its 18 ProTour licenses. The UCI calculates sporting value by looking at team riders' placings over the previous two years plus a nebulous reckoning of, as the UCI puts it, "ethical, financial, and administrative criteria." On the sporting values graph, Slipstream sits in fourth position, almost equal to three higher-ranked teams: Leopard-RadioShack, BMC, and Sky. This graph is the one that matters. Fall off the rankings, and team sponsors say good-bye to the Tour de France and most other races that count.

Another slide highlights a line from the movie *Moneyball*: "We're not New York. Find players with the money that we do have." Clicking the slide brings up the trailer from the Brad Pitt flick about how the Oakland A's baseball franchise used a small budget and innovative, data-driven hiring to beat very wealthy, but more tradition-bound teams like the New York Yankees.

Vaughters would rather have Yankee-sized numbers. But given that in September, potential sponsor

ABOVE Steady performers like Tyler Farrar (here at Paris-Roubaix) deliver valuable UCI points to Slipstream. RIGHT A race that matters, the Tour of Flanders.

BigMat, a French version of Home Depot, pulled out at the last minute from a co-title deal Matt Johnson had been negotiating since April, he has to work with what he has.

Then Vaughters dives into the team's budget breakdown. Rider salaries consume 74 percent of the funds. The remainder covers race expenses, vehicles, staff wages, and anti-doping testing. A note on this slide points out that most teams dedicate about 64 percent of their monies to rider salaries. So that his riders know where the cash comes

from, the presentation shows revenue sources: 71 percent from sponsors, 8 percent from product merchandising on the team's Web site, and the rest from race appearance fees and team owner Doug Ellis.

The Slipstreamsports.com income is a growing component of the team's financial health. Thanks in part to the team's close connection with its followers, annual Web sales revenue has gone from zero to nearly $1.5 million in three years. Vaughters points out that the sales of team jerseys, bottles, and bikes are plowed back to the team's operations. He makes it clear that there is a straight line from the riders' own financial well-being to the sponsors they represent and the fans they interact with.

Another page in the presentation starts with a Herman Melville quote: "We cannot live only for ourselves. A thousand fibers connect us with our fellow men," then covers Paris-Roubaix and the Tour de France team time trial. The slide is more than a sentimental reverie. Vaughters is making a nuts-and-bolts point: Teamwork focused at the right races makes a quantifiable financial and sporting impact. In 2012, one such target is a new world championship team time trial event.

TOP LEFT It's pro riders, not amateurs, that fans come to see. TOP RIGHT Ryder Hesjedal and Christian Vande Velde on the Champs-Élysées. BELOW European cycling tradition runs deep and changes slowly.

Significantly, the new TTT is for trade teams, not national teams. As the Garmin folks discussed back in April in the Dolce Chantilly hotel lobby, a rainbow jersey from a world championship win generates exponential exposure boosts. "Let's play out the odds here," Vaughters suggests while brainstorming his presentation. The likelihood of Philippe Gilbert winning the 2012 road world championships that will be held on the same course where he won the Amstel Gold Race in 2010 and 2011 is good, but still a big gamble. The odds are "not one in two, I can tell you that," Vaughters says. "That's just impossible with 200 guys at the start. You could get a flat tire in the last kilometer." Odds on the street have Gilbert at 1 to 8. At the same time, Gilbert's cost to his new team, BMC, is high, reportedly in the $4 million range.

Meanwhile, Vaughters believes that there are two serious contenders for the world TTT crown: Garmin-Cervélo and BMC. "So, what is the probability of this team of riders winning the world

Johan Vansummeren's Paris-Roubaix win delivers big exposure for sponsors.

championship? Well, it's about one in two." Much better odds.

This is where teamwork and economics dovetail. If Gilbert wins the 2012 world championship road race (where he'll be riding for Belgium), "Is BMC the world champion?" Vaughters asks. "No. Philippe Gilbert is the world champion." On the other hand,

"What happens when Garmin-Cervélo wins the inaugural world team time trial championship? People say, 'Garmin-Cervélo is the world championship team.'"

"The six guys that actually ride the world team time trial championship will probably have a total overall payroll of about, eh, 2.5, 2.2 million euros, around there," Vaughters continues. So, at a cost far below one superstar's salary, Slipstream has an exponentially higher probability of landing the rainbow jersey—a prestige that isn't bottled up with one rider and his country, but spills over onto 29 riders and all the sponsors.

Of course, there is risk in telling your team riders that they work for a cheap squad compared with Gilbert's cash-flush employer. But there is no way around it, so Vaughters simply lays out the facts, even including an Emily Brontë quote on one slide that reads, "Honest people don't hide their deeds." Vaughters almost relishes his position as the Oakland A's of cycling. "We are one of the most flat teams in the peloton," Vaughters explains of the team's points stash. "Most teams have, like, one guy that has 600 points. And then their second guy has like 90 and the third guy has 40 and their fourth guy has 20 and their last guy has 10."

Garmin-Cervélo is not like that. In fact, five of its riders have 100 WorldTour points or more at the end of the season, starting with Martin at 286 and rolling down to Vansummeren at 100. "No other team has that depth," Vaughters proudly reveals. "And while sometimes it makes race selection difficult and it makes personalities and selecting strategies and tactics difficult, at the end of the day, we don't have a Cancellara, a Contador, a Cavendish, or a Gilbert. And unless you have one of those four riders, the only way you are going to be on top is to be stronger as a collective." Taking on the voice he will assume in front of his gathered riders, Vaughters expounds on his collective-power philosophy: "That keeps us in a position where our license, our position, our sponsorship, *your* paycheck are not ever at risk."

In creating the 2012 team mix, Vaughters does not extend Daniel Lloyd's contract for another year. He does, however, hire a 27-year-old Dutch rider named Thomas Dekker. Vaughters knows this hire is going to be controversial because Dekker admitted to using EPO throughout 2007 and 2008. How can Vaughters rationalize letting go of a certifiably clean rider and bringing on an admitted cheat? The presentation addresses this apparent values scuffle by pointing out that Dekker is just the sort of overlooked, inexpensive rider who will deliver steady results needed to keep the team in the upper tier of the sporting value rankings.

TOP A visit to sponsor DSM strengthens its ties to the team. BOTTOM Philippe Gilbert (shown here winning Liège-Bastogne-Liège) saw his value skyrocket over a stellar season.

Jonathan Vaughters preaches success through unity, sacrifice, and innovation.

Like David Millar, Dekker made bad choices, but owned up to them and served a two-year suspension. Vaughters has been testing the Dutchman all year, and he is clean. Vaughters is convinced Dekker will stay that way. Dekker is also an astonishing talent. Along with three Dutch national time trial titles, Dekker has won the Tirreno-Adriatico stage race and the Tour of Romandie. More tellingly, he placed third overall at the Tour of the Basque Country and top 10 at the Amstel Gold Race, Liège-Bastogne-Liège, and La Flèche Wallonne—the three hilliest, most difficult one-day races on the calendar.

A time-trialing ace, who can place third at the cruelly mountainous Basque Tour and in the top 10 at the Ardennes classics? Dekker is a points-generating machine. Seen in terms of his raw talent (though Dekker was stripped of his Ardennes classics results, doping alone would not account for the longevity and consistency of his results) and low cost (because he is tainted), getting Dekker into the Slipstream fold makes logical sense, especially when triangulated with longitudinal testing evidence that he is clean.

While hewing to data can make difficult decisions simpler for Vaughters, for those losing their livelihood and their mates who look on in dismay, they make him seem merciless. Some of the riders ask why he is letting Lloyd go. "He's such a nice guy," Vaughters paraphrases. "You bring in Thomas Dekker but then punt out my buddy?" Vaughters sighs. He understands this discontent; judging complicated humans by running them through a spreadsheet is cold. But, he says, "At the end of the day, my responsibility is to make sure that we have high-level performances for our sponsors. I need people who have the ability to do that." Another slide digs into this notion. What may seem unfair to one rider who doesn't have his contract renewed or doesn't get named for a favored race can also be seen as just and caring because it defends the livelihoods of the entirety of riders and staff. And more often than not, that means hiring and racing the people who will keep the team's rank high.

Vaughters is no fan of the UCI's sporting values system. He lets his riders know this in a slide that shows a statement of his from the minutes of the UCI's Professional Cycling Commission: "This points system is unacceptable to the teams in pro cycling, because it will destroy the fabric of teamwork and create a situation where riders are only concerned about their points and not their team, their ethics, nor their teammates." Vaughters doesn't like it, but it's the reality he's been dealt.

THOUGH THE TWO DON'T AGREE ON MANY things, UCI president Pat McQuaid endorses Vaughters's anti-doping crusade as step one to bringing the sport greater financial vitality. McQuaid, 62, has been the UCI president since

Canadian bikes, Canadian mechanic, New World team.

2006. He comes from a family of Irish cyclists and effuses a profound passion for the sport. McQuaid, who won the Tour of Ireland twice in the 1970s, observes that "Jonathan is definitely 100 percent for the sport and 100 percent to improve the sport."

"The most important fundamental priority of the teams is to deal with doping and get the credibility of our sport back," McQuaid tells me. In his opinion, once "the media recognizes our sport as credible and the fans recognize it as credible, then the spon-

sors will come in." Where McQuaid and Vaughters split is in their methods. "He has a vision which is somewhat coming from his American background," McQuaid points out. "He sees it should go in a certain way. I still have a European background." McQuaid adds, "We both have the same aims, the same objectives. But I'm in one area, and he's in another area, and both paths don't always go the same. Whilst they are both going forward, they crisscross from time to time."

183

TOP The TTT win puts a Tour stage in the pocket of nine riders. ABOVE The first pair of lions; five more to come. OPPOSITE The Tour defines the sport.

McQuaid sees cycling entering an era where dope-free riders attract multinationals keen to unlock new markets. "Hopefully in the next four or five years we'll have a race in all of the BRIC countries," McQuaid says of the UCI's desire to expand WorldTour races into Brazil, Russia, India, and China. All have huge populations and growing economies, which makes them attractive to advertisers. "We are very much going into a global phase," the Irishman explains. And with that "changing of the balance of events, the UCI would hope that when that comes about there will be new sources of revenues for the teams."

Montréal and Québec race organizer Serge Arsenault is one of these global bridges. Arsenault, 63, has been involved with cycling and television since 1974, when as a 26-year-old reporter for the Canadian Broadcasting Corporation he covered Eddy Merckx winning the world championships in Montréal. Starting in 1988, he organized a pro race in Montréal for five years. A few years ago he got back into cycling promotion. "This is my pleasure," the genial French Canadian says. After a career building his television networks, "I want to come back to what I love most, organizing and doing something for cycling."

Race promotion costs challenge the race organizer's business. "When you are WorldTour," Arsenault explains, "you have the obligation to invite the 18 ProTour teams." And that includes about $25,000 per team for spending money, their hotels, food, and travel expenses. "We will have nearly two 747s to bring all the riders and the bikes and the mechanics."

"I hate to call that losing money," Arsenault says of the $4.5 million he spends on the Montréal and Québec races. "I'm calling that investing money." As a race organizer and television network operator, he knows both the supply and demand side of bike racing. He understands what a network needs to broadcast a compelling sports product, and he knows what a race organizer has to go through to produce such a product. "Money does not come along easy, just like that, boom, falling on the floor. Money comes with a product that you will guarantee."

In Arsenault's opinion, the lack of a reliable cycling TV product is the biggest challenge to dependable advertising dollars. And that comes

down to the disproportionality of the Tour de France. "I hope that the Tour of California, I hope that the Colorado race will be big, for one reason," Arsenault divulges. "The fact that the Tour de France is the only one on top, and a team lives or dies often by their success at just one competition clearly indicates that the sport is quite sick."

Because "the Tour is the only event that counts," cycling does not offer a multinational

sponsor a product that it can leverage throughout the year. "Tennis solved that problem 40 years ago when Wimbledon was nearly alone," Arsenault explains. Referring to the ATP World Masters series of nine tennis tournaments from Paris to Australia to the United States, he recounts how tennis created a cohesive international circuit. Of tennis, he proposes, "You don't ask yourself, 'Do you think that the Masters in tennis will be spon-

Even in the snarl of the support staging area, branding is a critical team function.

sored?' Gee whiz, they are *running* after tennis. But they guarantee their product, they guarantee TV worldwide." To be economically stable, he says, professional cycling "will have to do the same thing. And it will hurt the first time. But we have to make sure that cycling is something else than the Tour de France."

Vaughters has a similar vision. He argues that by rationalizing its calendar, pro cycling can better bridge their appeal to both advertiser-sponsors and recreational cyclists. "If you can tap into the recreational community," Vaughters says, "that's such an incredibly affluent and important body of people worldwide." Calling people who watch and ride bikes "the golden egg in cycling," Vaughters says, "You have the largest body of recreational athletes anywhere in the world out there participating in your sport." Yet, he adds, "none of them understand what's going on in the professional leg of the sport. If you want to make true fans out of people, engaged fans, they have to understand it." Today, the sport may be traditional, but it's not logical in a way that allows the mass of participants to grasp it. "You've got to keep the best aspects of that tradition and add in a bit of logic," he contends.

Vaughters proposes a racing structure where the top 12 or 15 pro cycling teams are required to appear in the same events, and that calendar leads to an overall prize at the end of the season. "It's got to be narrowed down, focused, engaged, simplified, cohesive." An understandable series of races leading up to a yearlong winner, Vaughters argues, will create drama and suspense. In turn, more viewers will consistently tune in. It will also make the sport accessible to more fans—followers who are cur-

rently bewildered by the sheer number of races and the seemingly arbitrary nature of their importance on the calendar.

That said, Vaughters cautions against turning cycling into a two-wheeled Formula One. "You have to make it cohesive and appealing to a broader audience while still keeping the quaintness of it," he notes. "You lose that, and the sport's dead." The person to make that change must have both the romantic's appreciation for cycling's grittily primitive tradition and the entrepreneur's nose for profit.

Ramunas Navardauskas, an example of Slipstream's faith in empirical evidence over canard.

ABOVE The timeless appeal of racing and riding.
OPPOSITE Thor Hushovd's value grew beyond
Slipstream's means.

sport is bound by the code of "this is the way it's always been done."

Today, cycling is "an unpolished diamond," Vande Velde says. "It's on the cusp of being really big." However, if the sport clings to the status quo, Vande Velde feels it will stagnate in its current state, which he calls "the biggest amateur sport in the world."

For Vande Velde, the UCI is not focused on the pro peloton. "It's reached the tipping point," he says of cycling's governing body. "We've outgrown the UCI." Pointing out that the UCI governs and promotes everything from BMX, to mountain biking, to trials riding, to track, to pro road racing, Vande Velde says the UCI's umbrella today would be as if the multibillion-dollar Formula One organization reported to an agency that also governed go-karting, NASCAR, Indy car racing, and soap box derby.

The Chicagoan is also frustrated by the riders' inability to take command of their own destiny— a future they really do own, since it's them, not a race organizer or UCI functionary the fans flock to France and Colorado to see. "Sometimes I feel like my hands are tied, and I wish I could have more of a part." He feels powerless. Referring to instances where riders believe the UCI has slipped doping results to the press before the accused rider has been afforded due process, Vande Velde says the lack of accountability disheartens him. "You're not mad, you're not upset, you're just frustrated."

Roger Hammond echoes a sentiment expressed by other team riders. Even if they have the desire and political will to become that rallying force, their sport is so physically taxing that they don't have the energy or time to take charge. "Cycling is a highly time-intensive sport," Hammond says. "I would love

riders, sponsors, and stakeholders. They just can't sit down at the table together.

For the riders, this is a disappointment and source of frustration. In Christian Vande Velde's opinion, the biggest challenge Vaughters faces in trying to change the sport for the better is "people who don't see the big picture, the people who have their little piece of the pie and are not willing to give it up and are not willing to sacrifice a little bit to maybe get a lot in the future." Vande Velde attributes much of that reluctance to tradition. The

to get involved with changing the way that cycling is organized. The problem is I just don't have the time."

Hammond graduated in 1996 with a university degree in materials engineering. He worked for a time for British Petroleum, researching the changing properties of steel for pipeline applications, and the engineer in him recoils at confounded systems. Of the UCI, he says, "How can you have a union that's representing the riders, who is also responsible for controlling the riders in a doping control way, and is also the body that is implementing the rules? And they also want to select the teams for the races?" He says with quiet exasperation, "It's just a huge, huge conflict of interest."

Discussing the riders' inability to unionize, Tyler Farrar says communication is one challenge. "It's very difficult to communicate across so many languages and cultures and financial situations." He continues, "You can't get everyone on that same page. People are coming from very different places. Some people are willing to really sacrifice some things this season, whereas other people they don't want to or can't afford to make those sacrifices." Financial expectations also play. "A well-paid American or western European rider's take on things is a lot different than the attitude of somebody from a really poor eastern European country," Farrar explains. "For them a minimum salary is already quite good. They are more likely to just go along with things."

That said, Farrar says communication among riders is better today than it was even a half-decade ago. "Only in the last few years has English really become the language of the pro peloton. Even when I became professional six years ago, it wasn't like that. Now it's the go-to language of

the peloton. Now the business of cycling is done in English. We had some riders' meetings at races to discuss the radios issue. The fact that you could have a meeting with every team represented because everyone had a language in common with English, it made life so much easier than trying to do it in multiple languages and not understanding and not trusting what was going on."

Finally, legal jurisdictions complicate devising a common riders' charter. "That's the biggest problem we run into with cycling," Farrar explains. "You are dealing with teams from America, from France, from Germany, from Belgium, from Spain, from Italy, from Russia, from Kazakhstan, from all over the world. So you try and push these things through and on top of the battle itself you get this whole other battle about under what jurisdiction does this fall? If this goes to court, does it go to court in France? Or does it go to court in America? The laws are different in each place. So if it goes to court in one place, then the outcome could be one thing. If it goes to court in another, it could be something else."

Matthew Pace knows courts. The New York attorney specializes in sports and has represented Slipstream from the beginning. He has negotiated for clients in the NFL to lacrosse, Major League Baseball to polo.

For Pace, the striking difference between the pro cycling business and other sports is that the people who assume the bulk of the financial risk do not enjoy a proportional return. "The model has evolved in a way which I think is very different from other sports, where the entities that are absorbing the risk do not have the opportunity to share in most of the reward." Pace points out that while football and baseball teams spend millions on salaries and travel, "they also have all the media rights, and they also have all of the ticket sales and event promotion rights. But that doesn't exist in cycling." In other words, while Doug Ellis and Vaughters are responsible for generating the cash to keep a team afloat, there has traditionally been no meaningful way to see a return on that investment of time and capital. "The riders and the equipment and the travel. That's all absorbed by the teams, and the only real sort of meaningful revenue opportunity is to sell sponsorships. That to me is the most unique thing about cycling."

In 2010 Pace visited Paris-Roubaix. The Roubaix velodrome is as iconic to cycling as the Indy 500 Brickyard is to car racing and Boston's Fenway Park is to baseball. Yet, he recalls being "amazed by the lack of sponsor signage." He marvels that "you saw mostly government agencies as the primary sponsors."

Pace feels this noticeably noncorporate patronage reflects a European sponsorship model. He cites NASCAR as an American model, where a govern-

ing body controls the sport and sanctions races, and teams exist as franchises. In NASCAR, teams share a portion of the general revenue generated by the sport as a whole. This type of structure, Pace opines, while "proving itself to be the most financially viable model for sport, has not yet really been applied to the business of cycling."

As for Ellis's influence on the sport, Pace says, "Doug put his name and his money and his hard work together with Jonathan to not just put together a team that could win races, but a team that sort of serves as a shining example for how to win races. It's impossible to argue that they have been anything but the sort of beacon leading this sport through a very dark time. Doug saw an opportunity to take

OPPOSITE Johan Vansummeren enters the Roubaix velodrome and the history books. ABOVE Tom Peterson follows Euro greats Ivan Basso and Andy Schleck in Colorado.

Andreas Klier says cycling needs heroes.

in how cycling's governing bodies enforce their rules. Examples are easy to find. Former Lance Armstrong domestiques Floyd Landis and Tyler Hamilton both accused the UCI of covering up test results for their teammate. And in 2002 and 2005, the UCI accepted $125,000 in donations from Armstrong while he was racing under the UCI's governance. While Armstrong and the UCI deny anything unseemly took place, Ford holds that as long as the perception persists that doping penalties are unfairly administered, the sport remains hobbled. "Until people think there is a more fair approach to that—and that all goes back to the governing body—that's a liability for sure."

TV commentator Paul Sherwen has been involved with cycling for more than three decades. The 2011 Tour de France was the 33rd the British broadcaster covered. Sherwen also raced seven Tours between 1978 and 1985. He sees changing demographics both inside and outside the pro peloton as an engine for change. "Cycling I think is a little bit like boxing. It was a sport that for many years got you out of the gutter, or got you out of the farm."

At the turn of the twentieth century, cycling grew in Europe because bicycles were affordable transportation for immigrant industrial workers. The cycling profession was, like boxing, a pugilistic, accessible way out of a brutish life in the mills of the Industrial Revolution. And because a bicycle was affordable on a workingman's salary, the doors to the sport were wide open. "Originally people rode bikes to get to work," Sherwen explains. "Now people ride bikes to get fit. Bikes in the old days were 100 [British] pounds. Now they are 6,000; 8,000; 10,000 dollars. It's seen as a white-collar sport now."

a sport that was going in the wrong direction and really step out and change the direction. There are very few people in the world that you can point to who have ever done that."

ESPN writer Bonnie Ford has a wide-angle view of global sports since she also covers Olympic events. Ford does not see doping as the main impediment to cycling's growth. In her view cycling has been more successful than most other sports in reforming drug problems. A barrier she does see, however, is a lack of transparency

This change is filtering into the peloton, too. "The level of intelligence of cyclists has increased dramatically from the postwar 50s and 60s," Sherwen says. "Nowadays there's a bunch of guys out there in the peloton who have got degrees."

As for an outsider reforming cycling, Sherwen says, "I don't see any reason at all why the teams don't leave and create their own Formula One. The UCI, I think, ought to be very careful. Not only the team owners could leave and set up their own infrastructure, ASO could leave; ASO could run their own calendar." Indeed, he points out, "You could take the top 15 teams in the world and set up a parallel circuit." That has not transpired yet, but "if the stars line up, and people believe that that is the future of the sport, they will make that step. They will make it happen at that point." The challenge Vaughters faces is, in Sherwen's words, "getting everyone to come to the table. At the end of the day, everybody wants to win. And to win, you have to be individualistic, and you have to be selfish. And so, being able to put that to one side, to get everybody to work together is probably the most difficult thing."

Difficult, but possible. As the Garmin-Cervélo team wraps up its season in Boulder by looking ahead to the next year, Serge Arsenault's words are a snapshot of the state of the business of pro cycling. "The base is there, the public is there." The public is every day more hooked on the intrinsic joy of watching and riding bikes. "We are just so near. We have the key. It's bizarre. It's like we have the lock in front of us, but we shadow our eyes. We have a good thing in our hands right now. The product is ready to go; pick it from the tree."

No one has more skin in the Slipstream game than team owner and financial underwriter Doug Ellis. Reflecting on the sport and its potential, Ellis says, "I don't own a franchise. I own a company that this year has a team." With the sport's current business structure, whether that team persists beyond the expiration of its current contract with Garmin through 2013 is subject to a host of variables, such as whether it qualifies for a ProTour license each year and whether, when a potential cosponsor like BigMat disappears, Ellis is willing to write a check to fill in the resulting budget shortfall. "I don't have a guaranteed piece the way I would if I was a Major League or NFL stakeholder," he explains. "And I think that that degree of certainty—knowing that I'm here today, I'm here next year, I'm here five years from now—that stability actually allows the value to go up and to make long-term commitments with partners."

As for how to reduce this fragility, Ellis says he has heard variations on the turn-cycling-into-F1 analogy from the day he entered the sport. He refers to past discussions where West Coast investors proposed buying up the sport in order to make a cohesive racing calendar and league. Paraphrasing their discussions, he says, "There used to be guys who would say, 'Let's buy up the sport. How much could it be? 100 million, 200 million dollars—we can do that.'" Ellis says these propositions are tone deaf to the "soft issues" that have to be accounted for when improving the sport's business stability.

"I think what they didn't understand is that if it's the wrong group of people who own the Tour, *there is no Tour*. You know, you can't do the Tour without

Few sports allow fan intimacy like pro cycling.

that allows teams to thrive in an environment that gives sponsors and investors confidence that they are buying into more than a chimera (such as what happened in 2011 with the dissolution of HTC-Highroad, the winningest team in pro cycling).

"I don't mean to come across as unambitious," Ellis says with unguarded frankness. "The point is not to make a lot of money. The point is maybe not to lose a lot of money. For me, I think that if we can run a program that essentially pays for itself through its sponsorship and other revenue—you know, Web sales, et cetera—for me, that's actually a huge success. We are not there, and I think if we could get there that would be a great success and incredibly gratifying. I would love that."

As for Vaughters, he's not ready to say whether the team has yet made a lasting difference in pro cycling. "I think we need to be a thorn in the side for a few more years for it to have a truly long-term and profound effect. We need to have longevity and sustainability before people start changing as a result of us being a constant nuisance." The irony, he points out, is that the structural changes he and Ellis see as fundamental to both their team's and pro cycling's long-term health take time. Chuckling at his role in a catch-22, Vaughters says, "We have to prove that we can be around a long time so that we can actually change the system so that we can be around a long time."

the French government policing the entire country for an entire month. It is a national treasure, and the national treasure isn't just going to be subject to business laws. So I think that it all has to be done in a more cooperative, joint way."

Referring to the priceless cultural and historical value in races like the Tour and Paris-Roubaix, Ellis says of cycling, "We have actually a tremendous amount in place that is loved and whose history is valuable." The challenge is preserving these unquantifiable assets while also creating a business model

LEFT A new season unfolds where the team began: Boulder, Colorado. OPPOSITE The Argyle Armada.

INDEX

NOTES: *Italic page numbers indicate pictures. (When the caption and the picture are on different pages, both page numbers are cited, with only the page number for the picture in italics.)*

When articles or prepositions in foreign languages (le, la, van, etc.) occur in people's names, the name is alphabetized by the first letter of the article (e.g., Le Mével is alphabetized under L). When they occur in place names, restaurant names, etc., those names are alphabetized by the first letter of the first nonarticle word (e.g., El Ranxo is alphabetized under R).

ABOUT THE AUTHOR

Mark Johnson has covered cycling as a writer and photographer for national and international publications since the 1980s. His work has been published in cycling titles including *VeloNews* in the United States, *Cycling Weekly* in the UK, *Vélo* in France, and *Ride Cycling Review* in Australia as well as general-interest publications including the *Wall Street Journal* and the *San Diego Union-Tribune*. A category II road cyclist, Mark has also bicycled across the United States twice and completed an Ironman triathlon. He has a PhD in English literature from Boston University and has worked as a freelance writer and photographer for the Slipstream Sports cycling team since 2007. His other passion is surfing, which he does frequently from his home in Del Mar, California.

PHOTO BY JOEL WESTWOOD